Rediscovering *Public* Library Management

For Hazel

Rediscovering
Public Library
Management

Bob Usherwood
Reader in Librarianship, Department of Information Studies,
University of Sheffield

LIBRARY ASSOCIATION PUBLISHING
LONDON

© Bob Usherwood 1996

Published by
Library Association Publishing
7 Ridgmount Street
London WC1E 7AE

Library Associaton Publishing is wholly owned by The Library Association.

First published 1996

British Library Cataloguing in Publication Data
A catalogue record for this book is available from the British Library

ISBN 1-85604-175-1

Typeset from author's disks in 10/13pt Aldine 401 by Library Association Publishing
Printed and made in Great Britain by Bookcraft (Bath) Ltd, Midsomer Norton, Avon

> 'the public sector really is different from the private sector, and all those ideas about reinventing government to bring in management practices of private enterprise are just cocktail party chatter'.
>
> Leonard Wrigley and David McKevitt, 1994

Contents

Acknowledgements

T HANKS ARE DUE to all those librarians who gave their time to respond to the questionnaire distributed as part of the preparation for this text. Particular thanks are owed to Martin Molloy, who helped with an earlier version of Chapter 7, and to Richard Proctor, an old professional friend and new colleague at the Department of Information Studies, for his thoughts on quality and much else, and for providing a practical perspective. As ever, the writing of this book has been helped by the stimulating environment provided by staff and students at the University of Sheffield. I also wish to acknowledge the contribution of members of the Aslib/DNH research team, and Margaret Evans, Eileen Milner and Gill Stroud, who worked with me on some of the research projects drawn on in the text.

Some parts of this book have been delivered as conference papers at professional gatherings and the reactions of various audiences have proved to be very valuable indeed. My thanks to them. I have tried to provide references for all writers whose words I have used in the text. I apologize to any I may have unconsciously used without due credit, but am pleased to acknowledge my general debt to the literature. Thanks also to Helen Grindley for providing an index and to Helen Carley for her lightly given but persuasive advice, and to all the staff at L A Publishing.

None of this, or indeed my other work, could have been achieved without the constant support of my daughters, Julie and Tania, and my wife Hazel. They have managed me in the best sense of the word.

Bob Usherwood
Sheffield
November 1996

Personal prologue

THIS BOOK IS written by someone who believes that good management is essential to the effective delivery of our public library services. It is not, however, a 'how to' book, and it is not intended to repeat at length the work that can be found in the standard texts on library management. There are many general works, and others more specific to the library field, in which readers can find illustrations and discussions of those dimensions of management that are shared by a variety of organizations.

In common with many colleagues in library education and in the profession, the author believes that librarians must be prepared for management responsibilities. There is a need for public library managers and prospective public library managers to be familiar with such things as systems theory, and/or the social action approach to the study of organizations. They need to be aware of the implications of different organizational structures; to know the importance of goals and evaluation; to have considered management tasks, roles and styles; and to be aware of the impact of organizational power and conflict and the value of leadership. The professional librarian must be an effective communicator, be aware of group dynamics and have decision-making skills. He or she must be concerned with organizational development, marketing and financial management, and possess the skills necessary to manage personnel in library and information services. These might include interviewing, counselling, coaching and appraisal skills. The good public librarian will know about communication practices, interpersonal skills, dealing with stress, staff training, motivation, job satisfaction and staff supervision.

These are the kinds of topics that are taught at professional seminars and on management courses in our library schools, and it is right that they should be. The text you are about to read, as the above should confirm, is not intended to be a tirade against management as such, but rather a discourse on some of the sins that have been committed in management's name. Sins, I would argue, that have been committed largely as a result of ideological fervour rather than a belief in the effective delivery of public services. Indeed, one might suggest that some of the new managerialist ideas have been introduced because of a dogmatic disbelief in any kind of delivery of public service. I do not, then, question the value of management: indeed, I recognize its importance in equipping public librarians to deal with a changing world. I do, however, question the new managerialism.

Managerialism 'is a set of beliefs and practices, at the core of which burns the seldom-tested assumption that better management will prove an effective solvent for a wide range of economic ills' (Pollitt 1993). Although its roots can be traced back to so-called scientific management and the work of Frederick Taylor (1911), its more recent origins 'have been attributed to New Right ideology and the advent of the "new politics" ' (Farnham & Horton 1996a). I am particularly concerned at the ideological spin that has been introduced in recent years. In effect, what is essentially a political dogma has been justified by spurious references to good management. Contracting out, privatization and performance-related pay are just three examples of this.

The public service professional needs management skills. The public librarian requires such skills to deliver social results, and nothing that is said in this book is intended to question the value of management concepts *per se*. I do, however, argue that those management skills and techniques need to be considered in the context of public service, a context, I would maintain, that is in many ways quite different from that to be found in the private sector. It is my intention to examine the implications of these theoretical concepts for the competent and creative management of public libraries in the hope that readers will explore their own responses to some key issues.

The aim of the text you are about to read is to examine the appropriateness of private sector management techniques and values to the delivery of a public library service. In so doing it will make use of original research specifically undertaken for this publication. A questionnaire based on that used by Talbot (1994) was sent to every chief public librarian in the United Kingdom. For a postal survey it achieved a high response rate of 69%, and I should like to thank those colleagues who responded to what was a fairly lengthy document. Because so many gave their opinions the data collected and presented are an accurate reflection of the current perceptions of senior library professionals. The book also utilizes original data, many not published before, from other projects with which I have been involved. These include work on the Library Association Standards, a British Library funded project on TQM, the DNH Public Library Review, and personal research on elected members.

I have also tried to make use of a wider range of ideas than are to be found in the populist management texts to be seen on the shelves of airport bookshops. In recent years the populist approach appears to have had a considerable influence on the practice of public management. For instance, academics (Gunn 1987) have noted the links between the Audit Commission's emphasis on the infamous three Es and Peters and Waterman's best sellers. The ideas of these two writers have been very influential but also, as Guest (1992) has demonstrated, 'dangerously wrong'.

Although such texts are clearly important 'as a source of rhetoric, because local government professionals increasingly want to define their roles in a way that fit private sector business models, it is less clear how effectively they will be translated into practice' (Cochrane 1993). Until recently, 'both in public debate and scholarly writing the vague concept of "management" in the private sector has been borrowed more or less uncritically' (Kooiman & Eliassen 1987). It is my belief that the time has come to question many of the present conventional wisdoms, at least so far as they apply to public libraries. It is my hope that public librarians and those responsible for public library policies, together with students of librarianship, will be encouraged by the arguments and data presented to consider the issues raised.

Those who take a different view from the author would point out that there is a body of literature on consumerism and marketing that argues that with libraries, as with other services, the customer should be regarded as King or Queen. Indeed, one of the objectives in writing this book is to invite professional colleagues to consider the similarities and differences between the public and private sectors, the customer and the citizen. The political environment of the past decade means that we need to place the pressures of consumerism in context and recognize that public libraries have a public purpose as well as a duty to the individual user.

Managing a public library, like managing any public service, is different from and arguably more difficult than managing a supermarket or a small business. To insist that any one model of management – and these days it is invariably the private sector model – contains the absolute and essential truth 'is not only intellectually limited but contrary to good management practice which requires, the flexible application of models with due considerations for the aims, structures and ethos of any particular organisation' (A. M. Roberts 1993).

The early announcement of this book advertised it as a re-evaluation of public library management. However, through the process of reading and thinking about the literature and reviewing the data received from librarians it gradually became a personal rediscovery of public purpose. In fact, that journey of rediscovery had started a little earlier, with my involvement with the DNH Public Library Review. It soon became clear that many of the issues to be considered in this text had also been of concern to the Aslib team. I should emphasize that the chapters that follow provide an individual viewpoint and are not connected with the Review in any official way. However, because of the potential significance of the PLR, and to help put the present text in context, I have included, in the Appendices, a brief personal perspective on the research that led to the Aslib recommendations.

Reviewing the data collected for this study and recalling the debates that surrounded the DNH Review, it became clear that we do not need to re-evaluate or even reinvent what we do, but rather we need to rediscover our public purpose. In particular we need to rediscover the *public* in public library management. I maintain and argue, in this text, that there is a difference between public and private purposes. Moreover, despite our present difficulties I believe that public library management is not only different but also potentially more rewarding.

Part 1

Where are we now?

In the public sector the combination of centralised expenditure control, even tighter spending limits and the standardisation of performance measures has afflicted all kinds of public provision, from the quality of public libraries to the very survival of recreation grounds.

WILL HUTTON, *The State we're in*, 1996

There are two particularly indicative instances of market-led inadequacy, the Public Libraries and Broadcasting. Since this range of governments took over, the Public Library system has been under unfriendly pressure.

RICHARD HOGGART, *The way we live now*, 1995

Chapter 1

What have we done – the end of the public service?

'M ANY OF US have a vague "feeling" that things are moving faster . . . among many there is an uneasy mood – a suspicion that change is out of control' (Toffler 1970). Alvin Toffler's statement of over a quarter of a century ago will strike a chord with many public librarians. Members of the profession, in common with many other groups in the public sector, have faced major changes in recent years. When the present author was a Chief Librarian in the mid-1970s the public library world had barely heard of CCT, internal markets, contracting out, market testing, performance-related pay and other words from the lexicon of the new managerialism.

Moreover, since that time, or more correctly 1979, the government has introduced no fewer than 210 Acts that have affected the functions, responsibilities and shape of local government. At the same time, gurus of the new management have introduced one new technique after another, some of which have been of doubtful validity. Managers have been encouraged to believe that solutions can be found in one minute (Blanchard 1994), or that they should thrive on chaos (Peters 1988). Such ideas had much in common with the shallow nature of the decade in which they were born, but it is now becoming clear that, to a large extent, they were part of the problem rather than a solution. People can only take so much chaos.

In the public library field, as more than one researcher has discovered, there has been a move 'away from the "community librarianship" models which characterized the profession in the 1970s and early 1980s. Declining public expenditure over the last 14 years has forced public libraries to boost their income-generating activities as a means of replacing that funding' (Eastell 1994).

Such a direction was advocated by the Adam Smith Institute (1986) over a decade ago, when it stated that 'It is only through charging economic prices and competing for customers in the market place that the real level of public demand for goods and services can be determined and a proper allocation of resources made'. In *Ex Libris* and other publications they advocated a minimalist state and argued that the free market should operate within the public sector. The dangers of such dogma have been outlined by a number of writers, who are concerned that 'the emphasis of many market-style reforms is to take the public out of public services' (Parston 1994). Despite such criticism public librarians, like others in the public sector, have been encouraged to use private sector management techniques in order to bring such 'reforms' about.

In the years following the publication of *Ex Libris* the government published a series of discussion papers on the way public libraries should be managed. These were very different in tone from what had gone before. Official concern moved away from services to the disadvantaged to a methodology for costing public libraries, a manual on performance indicators and a guide to objective setting (Office of Arts and Libraries, 1990, 1991). At the end of 1995, in a statement to Parliament, the National Heritage Secretary was still linking good management with practices in the private sector. Despite two reports clearly demonstrating the case against contracting out, she concluded that 'Government is continuing to consider steps that might be taken to encourage more effective management of public libraries and to involve the private sector more in providing library services' (Bottomley 1995, 1996). There has, then, been a 'shift in the national political perceptions of libraries, from the welfare oriented service that was accepted up to the 1970s, to the idea that libraries should become part of an "enterprise culture" ' (Evans 1991).

For those involved in the day-to-day management of public services it is tempting to see these changes as a purely British phenomenon. Indeed, this view has been encouraged by government spokespersons who have sought to market them as a British export. However, although change has been a factor in public services across the world, as a recent OECD report (1992) demonstrates, there is little agreement as to the appropriate type of change. Basically, the OECD identified two major trends: decentralization, whereby greater power is given to local government and market orientation whereby services are modelled on, or even transferred to the private sector. Some countries, such as Belgium and France, have sought to combine the two.

In Britain there can be little doubt that the change in the structure and style of local government management has been greatly influenced by the policies of the Thatcher and Major administrations. This view is supported by the Chief Librarians surveyed for this study. As Figure 1.1 shows, 86% of respondents believed that new policies imposed by central government had been a major force for change in the past five years.

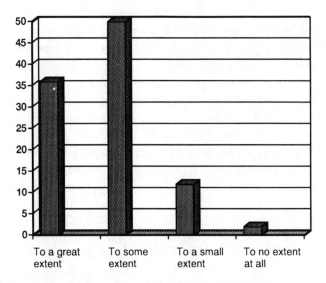

Fig. 1.1 *Forces for change: new policies imposed by central government*

In addition, many ideas have been imported from the United States which is, it should always be remembered, a very different culture and one where the principles of the market are much more widely accepted. It is a country in which the welfare state is almost a term of abuse and there is no major party of the Left. There are also constitutional differences. The American States are more powerful than British local authorities and have a narrower range of responsibilities.

It is a tenet of the new managerialism that the users of public services should be treated in much the same way as the customers of private business. Now, although there is nothing inherently wrong with 'customer care' and all that it entails, many (the present author included) would argue that this and other commercial attitudes can, when put into unthinking practice, present a challenge to the established public service ethic.

There has for some time been a feeling of unease beneath the surface froth of conference presentations and the management literature to be found in the professional press. For example, letters received by the author following the publication of a paper in *Public library journal* which commented on some librarians' uncritical acceptance of the enterprise culture (Usherwood 1992), suggested a distinct feeling of disquiet among a number of library professionals. As the distinguished correspondent Mark Tully (1993) said of another public service institution, the BBC, 'there is a very real sense of fear among staff which prevents them speaking their minds'. In a recent radio interview, a speaker from the Industrial Society spoke of the style of management that sets bullies on targeted people within organizations. It was suggested that the targets for such techniques are often good workers who seek to resist change. Closer to home, at a recent industrial tribunal a librarian alleged that she was 'bullied for five years', had an 'intolerable workload' placed on her, and was told to work late on the day that her mother died of cancer (Freely 1996). In our own field, as in others, there is very little evidence in the management literature on the use of such coercive strategies. However, as the above examples show, this does not mean that they are not happening, only that they have not yet been the subject of empirical research.

The private correspondence referred to above suggests that the public library world is not entirely free from such behaviour, as the extracts reproduced below indicate. For obvious reasons the people concerned are not identified. One person wrote:

> You have said so many things that I wanted to say, but because of personal circumstances, I have been too close emotionally to what is happening in many public libraries to make rational statements without personal bias. I could certainly have occupied a senior post in ★★★★'s new structure, [but] I did not feel that I could be an honest employee by taking part in an enterprise in which I could not invest a whole-hearted commitment. I . . . find it personally hard to accept the management philosophies of the 80s.

Another correspondent said:

> The ideology . . . is already causing a lowering of standards. . .I am only grateful that I don't have long to go before retiring myself. Why no protest? Because people are terrified of losing their jobs.

A conversation with a Chief Librarian confirmed that such feelings were not uncommon. He recognized the circumstances identifying 'career limitation' as the fate of those not willing to subscribe to the new orthodoxy. In this context 'career limitation' is an euphemism on par with that of 'collateral damage', as used by Gulf War generals.

The military analogy is not entirely misplaced. Indeed, a military 'hearts and minds' model is now advocated as a way of restructuring commercial organizations. Davies (1995) writes, 'Experience has shown that there is a very close match between the problems which have been presented in various military scenarios and the challenges of organizational change in the commercial field'.

This military theme was continued, albeit in a very different sense, by one Chief Librarian responding to the questionnaire used in the present study. He said:

> Here it would be pointless – and impossible – to resist the forces for change and we have therefore concentrated on channelling them and shaping our response as best we may to protect services and maintain staff morale. Even

so, right now I feel as if I'm in charge of a front line battalion in the Great War. (County Librarian)

This, it should be said, was a statement from an understanding and empathetic Chief. However as, Professor Martines has observed, some other librarians who once had respect for the English language now produce reports which read 'like an edict from some military GHQ' (Martines 1993).

The same misuse of language can also be heard on our professional platforms. Not so long ago, at a professional gathering, the author sat through an embarrassingly awful presentation by a speaker who sounded like, and promoted the ideas of, a dubious market trader. A little later, at another professional conference, speaker after speaker enthusiastically endorsed contracting out, privatization and the importation of commercial values. More worryingly, most members of what was a largely young and junior professional audience seemed to share the speakers' enthusiasms.

These and similar experiences have brought home the degree to which the ideology driven administrations of recent years have sought to interfere with professional, cultural and academic life. According to William Waldegrave, the government has 'introduced the entrepreneurial spirit into the corridors of power' (Waldegrave 1992). Students of the Scott report will no doubt have their own views as to the effect of this on government. In our own field, to quote one respondent :

The concept of the 'public service ethos' has been severely damaged by the Government – and locally by its myopic supporters – since 1979. The constant attacks on local government through the removal of its powers, its influence and scope for decision making has gone a long way to create a local administration in place of local government. This affects the way staff at all levels look at themselves and their job in the organization. They are weary of the political and financial environment in which we exist, and in such circumstances recognizing and making ethical choices is extremely difficult. (County Librarian)

Thus decent professional librarians have been driven on to the back foot by what Dennis Potter (1993) called 'the ideology-driven malice of ruling politicians'. There is, as we have already seen, a lot of fear about. Unfortunately we 'now live in a bullying, bitchy, conformist [society] where dissent from the prevailing philistine vulgarity rarely goes unpunished' (Billington 1993).

The entire basis of the public service ethos has been under continual attack for the past 16 years. To quote Farnham and Horton (1993), 'the key values which underpin New Right thinking are individualism, personal freedom and inequality, in contrast to those of collectivism, social rights and equality associated with the Keynesian Welfare State'. Moreover, the current members of the Conservative government are unable to understand the motivation of those who work in the public services. Those currently in charge believe 'that human beings are motivated purely by rational self-interest. Nobody is likely to bend his or her back save for the prospect of profit or high salary'. (Prisoners of Tory mistrust, *Independent on Sunday* 1995).

This attitude is also reflected in the New Right's attitude to the trade unions. Nicholas Ridley made no secret of this when he observed that 'the root cause of rotten local services lies in the grip which local government unions have over the services in many parts of the country . . . our competitive tendering provisions will smash that group once and for all' (quoted in McCarthy et al 1992).

In addition, we have seen 'a determined attack by the government on the professions . . . which were portrayed as conspiracies against the market' (Greenhalgh et al. 1995). This is true of the attacks from the Right, but we should also recognize that the far Left had little time for them either. Whereas the Right thought the market could provide, the Left put a rather simplistic faith in the community and/or saw professions as a conspiracy against the people.

As Figure 1.2 shows, in the opinion of Chief Librarians responding to this study the use of private sector techniques has increased, despite the fact that there is growing evidence to suggest that the success of their use has been somewhat limited. Whitley (quoted in Pollitt 1993), for instance, argues that 'Where judgment and discretion are involved in complex tasks which are highly context dependent skills are much more specific to particular situations and organizational fields. Here industry knowledge and personal networks are often crucial to effective management and skills are often not readily transferable.'

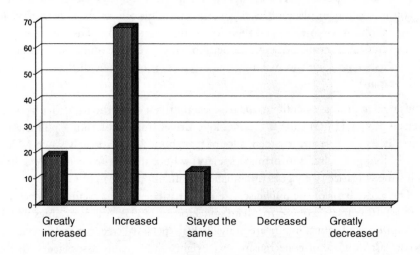

Fig. 1.2   *Use of private sector management techniques*

In addition, Kirkpatrick and Lucio (1995) observe that private sector 'ideas have been widely circulated amongst public sector managers through training programmes and appraisal schemes. [but] It is less certain . . . how far they were successfully implemented or how willingly.' Certainly such ideas have been widely circulated in the public library sector. Topics such as project management, public relations and decentralized budgets have been the subject of staff development programmes and, as Figure 1.3 indicates, the senior librarians responding to this study were largely satisfied with training provision in such areas.

More generally 'in the arts world we saw a "Thatcherite revolution . . . posing the question are we able to treat the arts like some form of commercial enterprise?" ' (Fowler 1994). People who have studied that question suggest not: indeed, they argue against the idea that the public sector is inherently bad and that the private sector provides a perfect role model. Professor Boylan of City University is of the opinion that: 'If British manufacturing had been a quarter as well managed as the arts since 1945, it would be ahead of the Japanese' (quoted in Fowler 1994). In addition, members of many public service professions have, to little or no avail, pointed out the damage caused by the uncritical adoption of private sector management philosophies. In the health service resignations have increased threefold as doctors have complained of a managerial culture, and at the BBC the 'ambivalence and doubt, where you pretend to be the commercial business that you cannot be, has led to the present near fatal crisis' (Potter 1993).

Commercial enterprises and public services are underpinned by different assumptions and values. The motivation for public service is just that, whereas for commerce it is profit, customer demand, competitive advantage and value

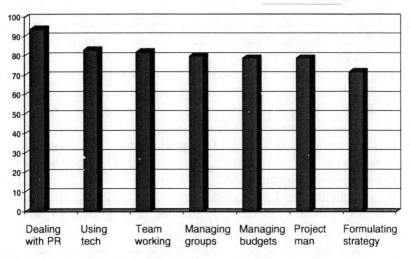

Fig. 1.3 *Satisfaction with provision for staff development in management techniques*

added. Whereas commercial firms seek to identify areas that will provide profitable markets for their products, public sector organizations are more concerned with identifying areas of need and deprivation, with a view to targeting specific services towards them. In the words of a leading public librarian, 'the management of any enterprise flows from the nature of the institution to be managed. Making sound management decisions for public libraries depends on a thorough understanding of the nature of the public library' (Curley 1994). 'Managerialism', says one academic librarian, 'is not concerned with notions like "the public good". Instead, it is concerned with obtaining organisational success in a competitive market' (Heery 1995). Haywood (1995) is equally trenchant in his views as to what is happening to public libraries. He concludes: 'the writing is on the wall', and that the thrust towards privatization and contracting out, as in Brent, will mean that the 'values of the dealing room will have finally demolished what (has) taken half a dozen Acts of Parliament and over 140 years of liberal legislation to establish.'

None of this means that public librarians cannot learn from the best experience in other public or private organizations, or that they cannot learn from us. For example, Osborne and Gaebler (1992), in their highly influential *Reinventing Government*, cite a librarian as 'their favourite practitioner of customer oriented government'. However, when their example is looked at more closely, what they describe has a great deal in common with good old community librarianship. They tell us that:

> One of the first things she did when she took over was to survey her customers. The survey told her that the libraries were neglecting two important groups: children and ethnic minorities.

Apart from the use of the private sector rhetoric, illustrated by the word 'customer', this could have been a description of Lambeth or many other authorities in the mid-1970s.

There is perhaps some support here for the views of those who have argued that there is little difference between management in the private and public sectors. Obviously one would not wish to argue with management techniques that emphasized the importance of listening to the user, or the better use of complaints and suggestions' procedures, or the development of more responsive professionals who seek to provide better physical and psychological access to the services they provide. Certainly we should not reject what may be sound practical ideas simply because they are associated with the ideology of a particular political party. On the other hand, we must be aware of ideas that have been introduced for reasons of ideology rather than sound management. As we shall see in the next chapter, there is a relationship between management and political values. In the context of the present debate we need to ask 'Have the new public management class (consciously or unwittingly) allowed themselves to become vehicles for a particular narrow set of political values?' (Isaac-Henry et al. 1993).

A word of caution against oversimplistic comparisons with the private sector comes from a rather surprising source. Researchers in the Cabinet Office warn that:

> Comparison with the private sector has to be treated with caution. In the private sector there is a direct relationship between commercial success – as measured by profitability and market share – and the standard of customer service. The public sector position is more complicated and in many instances distinctly different. In general the reasons for providing a service in the first place, the nature of that service and the manner in which it is delivered, are not dictated by markets. In these circumstances the balance between public expectations and the level of service to be provided is decided on the basis of political judgments about economic and social priorities. (Cabinet Office: Office of the Minister for the Civil Service 1988)

It is, then, in the words of Stewart and Walsh (1992), a mistake 'to assume that there is one approach applicable to public services based on an oversimplified model of the private sector'.

This should not come as a surprise to practitioners or academics in the field. Yet for some time now it has been fashionable both in practice and in theory to promote a generic model of management, and to maintain that the differences between the public and private sectors were little more than cosmetic. It remains something of a puzzle as to why such views have prevailed. Pollitt (1993), however, is of the opinion that:

> The attempt to impose a largely generic and neo-Taylorian model of management on the public services seems to have been either an act of culpable ignorance on the part of those concerned or an exercise in (possibly unwitting) ideological imperialism, or some mixture of the two.

Whatever the truth of the matter, it is perhaps useful to rehearse once again the fundamental differences between the public and private sectors. Over 40 years ago the economist Paul Samuelson (1954) distinguished public goods, which are collectively used by large numbers of people, from private goods, which are individually exchanged in the marketplace. Moreover it is clear that a public benefit can also result from the consumption of such goods. Although obviously not everyone uses a public library, what economists term 'important external economies or spillovers' are generated by those who do. The fact that, at some time, 60% of the population (Aslib 1995) use a public library helps our society to become more literate, better educated, more technologically developed, more productive and more politically stable. Such a society benefits all. However, equally obviously, a local authority, or for that matter a central government, could not finance the public library by selling that good and stable society to individuals in the marketplace. The library has to be publicly provided as a public good.

There is also an ethical and legal base to public service. This places some emphasis on such issues as fairness, equality and democracy. 'Democracy', says Rutter (1980), 'is the very foundation of professional local government management'. Thus as a part of local government public libraries have a political element. They are organizations that seek to serve and promote the common interest, and this has to be reflected in the values of those who manage them. Equity requires particular management processes. Most commercial managers will take some account of ethical and legal principles, but their main objective is to maximize profit. The public librarian not only has to work within such legal and ethical constraints, but often has to do so with limited resources. Her or his objectives will not be profit based but may include such intangibles as the promotion of literature, the interests of the local community and the broader needs of society.

The private sector model takes no account of the realities of political control. There is no equal of the elected member in private business. Over 50 years the literature of librarianship (Savage 1942; Usherwood 1993a), not to mention that of local government in general (e.g. Baddeley 1988), has shown that relating to politicians is a key skill for the public librarian. Today, 'in the overtly politicized environment in which librarians now function, the political skills that chief librarians need to meet this challenge are more than ever relevant' (Evans 1991). The public librarian is concerned with achieving objectives that have been determined by political processes.

Politics is a fact of life for the public library manager, as the need to make a profit is a condition for the manager of a commercial organization. As Ranson and Stewart (1994) observe, 'the task of management in the public domain is to enable political judgment'. Too often this task is seen in a negative light. Note how many writers who seek to introduce commercial ideas refer to libraries and similar institutions as 'not for profit' rather than, say, 'public service organizations'.

Whereas the public library service is concerned with the redistribution of the wealth of information, a private sector company has to be concerned with making a profit. At the very least, profit is a first among equals of the objectives of a commercial organization. Considerations such as market share, prestige and public profile might also be important, but in the long run it is the bottom line that plays the major part in the management strategy of the private sector. Unlike the public sector, 'the private sector can write off sections of the market because they are unlikely to be profitable' (Flynn 1993).

A public service is required to respond to needs rather than wants or demands. The difference is far more than semantic. In the first place, it is much more difficult to find evidence of need than a want because a person may not be aware of their need. Even if they are, they may not want what they need. Thus I might visit a doctor because I want some happiness pills, but I might really need to go on a diet or take more exercise. The public service professional has the responsibility to respond to need. If the library is, as the library at Alexandria once proclaimed, a hospital for the mind, then the public librarian has the responsibility to respond accordingly and not just provide the bibliographical equivalent of happiness pills.

The private sector manager is accountable only to company shareholders. Public accountability for the public library manager is rather more complex. He or she is accountable to a wide range of constituencies. These might include elected members, national politicians, council taxpayers, the Audit Commission, the local government ombudsman and the individuals and groups who make up the public that use or could use the service. 'The manager in the public sector operates within the goldfish bowl of public scrutiny and accountability' (Lawton & Rose 1994), and this is something that often surprises those who travel from the private to the public sector.

As readers' own experiences will confirm, the accountability of the market and contracts is not a replacement for public accountability. For instance, with the new privatized utilities it is increasingly difficult for a user to find anyone who will take responsibility: one is passed on from one source to another. If you contact the Regulators they will simply say that this is a function of the market. The water companies, the electricity companies and the rest have delivered large dividends to their shareholders, but have failed to deliver satisfactory services to their customers. Complaints against British Gas doubled in 1995 and there have been a record number of people complaining to the water companies. However, their 'customers' now have far less power to do anything about the situation than they had as citizens using a publicly owned utility.

Unlike a private firm, a public library has multiple and often competing goals. It is, after all, required by law to provide a comprehensive and efficient service. The objectives of a public library are multifaceted and not all of them are capable of being quantified. Moreover, in public organizations 'Activities are not . . . pursued for their own sake but to achieve public purposes, the outcome of which can only be fully tested in the public domain through public discourse' (Ranson & Stewart 1994). In the public sector an increase in supply leads to an increase in costs. The major incentive of the private sector manager to sell more and grow rich is rarely possible in a public service. Moreover, a public library delivers a service regardless of people's ability to pay.

The user of a public service is a citizen of a society rather than a customer in a marketplace. This is something that the New Right has great difficulty in understanding. For them there is no such thing as society: it is a collective idea that is alien to the individual concept of the market. For the public librarian, deciding who shall have access to what is the result of a political decision. It is the result of a collective choice regarding the provision for need in a community.

These different circumstances, many would argue, require different skills. At least one private sector consultant has admitted that in the public sector, 'on top of all the usual complexities of management, you have those of using public money, being politically accountable and working for the public good. It's like playing a game of three dimensions instead of two' (Bampfylde, quoted in Hassell 1993). There is support here for Whitley's (1989) opinion that 'managerial skills differ considerably from other sorts of expertise in their limited standardization across industries'. Of course there are superficial similarities between, say, the management of a supermarket and that of a public library, and there is no reason why some of these can not be translated into organizational systems and procedures, but given the differences in context, culture and communities outlined above, we need to ask if private sector techniques can be used 'wholesale' in the management of public libraries. Indeed, we need to ask if they should be used at all, and if they are, what will be their impact on the service and the people who use it? It is these and other questions that we shall consider in the text that follows.

Chapter 2

The politicians' view

A S HAS ALREADY been shown, public librarians are operating in a political – some would argue an increasingly political – environment. However, as Baddeley (1988) has written, too few managers in local government 'seem to have access to the mental world of politicians'. All too often the political dimension is left out of, or excluded from, the equation when the management of libraries is being discussed. This is a serious mistake, because if we are to persuade politicians that libraries are a public good that requires public funding, it is essential that we understand their motivation. This chapter will therefore discuss library management from the point of view of local politicians.

At the local level elected politicians are one of the prime decision makers so far as public library services are concerned, and their attitudes are important for the wellbeing of the service. In many respects those serving on the committees responsible for libraries have much in common with other councillors, although it would appear, if the figures from a recent study (Usherwood 1993a) are compared with those presented in the Widdicombe Report, that they are likely to have a higher level of education and are more likely to be in professional employment. The data also suggest that library committees tend to have a greater proportion of members with a relatively short experience of council work, and a greater proportion of members who may be toward the end of their political career, than the population of elected members as a whole. Although the term 'library committee' will be used as a convenient shorthand in the text that follows, readers will be aware that public libraries are subject to many different patterns of control, and this is often reflected in the different names given to the committees responsible for the library service. The implications of these different structures are considered further in the next chapter.

Elected members in general have to fulfil a number of roles. They are representatives of the electorate, of their party, their community and the committees on which they serve. They may see themselves as watchdogs, managers, policy makers and/or problem solvers. The chairperson of any committee has additional responsibilities. In terms of the library committee these have been identified as follows (Usherwood 1993a):

- to be a spokesperson for, and an advocate of, the library service;
- to run the library committee meeting;
- to act as the political arm of the service;
- to provide direction for the service;
- to liaise between officers and members and between officers and the public;
- to maintain links with the chairpersons of other committees.

This list, taken together with the findings of the Maud Committee, provides a description of the chairperson's role that appears to be closely related to Mintzberg's (1980) analysis of the working roles of managers. The data also suggest that elected members expect the chief librarian to possess both managerial and professional skills. As Knowles (1988) has written:

> The relationship between committee chairman and departmental head can be very close . . . If the chairman is to evaluate the professional advice given to the committee he requires a knowledge of the person giving it, including 'the bent of his mind'.

In addition, members want their professional officer to have an outgoing personality, diplomatic skills and what might be termed political nous. In many respects the views of the elected members support the conclusions of the Local Government Training Board report (1987b) which stated that:

> The credibility of the chief officer comes to rest on . . . personality and competence: the ability to communicate effectively within the authority and to a wider public, the ability to defend his or her staff and budget.

Contrary to much conventional wisdom, the elected members who serve on library committees appear to hold professional advice in high regard. However, this finding has to be seen in the context of a few local authorities that have seen fit to appoint non-librarians to the post of chief librarian. Such events led that most perceptive observer of the library world, Edward Dudley, to comment:

> Attendance [by librarians] at a miasma of management courses hasn't been sufficient to cut much ice with the politicos of Kent and East Sussex. (Dudley 1991)

In the light of such appointments, the question of how far politicians' perceptions of the role of the chief librarian coincide with the professional view of that role, is one that is worthy of further investigation.

These days few commentators see an unambiguous dividing line between the role of elected members and that of library officers. Rather, they relate the functions of each to the expertise that is seen to reside in each group. The librarian – the professional – is widely perceived to have special knowledge and professional abilities, whereas the politician is seen to be elected on a political position. The librarian is thought of as the expert, whereas the members generally recognize their 'amateur' role. In general terms the officers are perceived to be an important source of advice and professional expertise. Members see it as their own role to decide and direct policy in line with political priorities, and to act as a conduit for complaints. However, most are aware of a considerable blurring of these functions, and in many ways echo the Bains Report, which stated that 'a rigid interpretation of the roles of one or the other defeats any attempt to create a sense of unity of purpose within an authority' (Bains 1972).

Most members do not want to be involved in the day-to-day running of the library service, but there are exceptions to this general rule. This is particularly the case when it comes to discussing stock selection and the content of displays and exhibitions. The evidence supports the views of Jones (1973) and Bains (1972) that elected members are concerned with publicly controversial, or potentially publicly controversial, and sensitive issues. There is a considerable degree of ambivalence on the part of councillors with regard to their role in stock selection and the choice of subject for library displays. Conservatives tend to be more concerned with 'politicization' of displays, whereas Labour and Democrat members are more worried about social or community issues.

Although it would be wrong to overemphasize the degree to which elected members involve themselves in these activities, the evidence suggests that in a significant number of cases they do influence the decisions of officers. This influence is sometimes direct but more often indirect, in that librarians are expected, as one politician explained, to be 'sensible enough not to put on anything that might upset politically or morally' (Conservative chairman of county council).

Elected members keep themselves informed about the needs and attitudes of the public in a number of ways. They or their families visit libraries; they ask, using a variety of methods, the opinions of users and constituents; they talk to library officers and make use of reports and documents emanating from central and local government. In seeking out information elected members tend to use sources which are close to their locality and part of their own experience. As Jones and Stewart (1985) suggest:

> Councillors visit, as part of the routine of their work, the schools, homes and housing estates for which they are responsible. They therefore make decisions about areas, institutions and people that are not names but are part of their experience Thus in local government there is more scope for elected representatives to make an impact on policy making. MPs who have served as councillors often express frustration at their lack of involvement in policy

making as back-benchers compared with their direct and significant contribution as councillors.

In a recent report on the information needs of elected members, LAMSAC stated that:

> The ultimate objective must be to provide just the right amount of information for decisions to be made quickly and correctly, particularly in terms of policy-making and allocation of resources for operational activity' (LAMSAC Officers Advisory Group nd.).

In respect of library services, few elected members mention using local government information services or similar 'formal' sources. In fact, we know relatively little about members' use of information sources. Dearlove (1973), for instance, has suggested, with respect to councillors' use of information, 'that theories of selective perception and cognitive dissonance are of importance'.

One respondent to the present study felt that:

> The opportunities for the public to comment on library services is influencing local authority members' decisions often in favour of the real needs of the community rather than the dictates of political dogma (English County).

Obviously the public can influence the views of elected members, and it is probable that their decisions are more often based on what is perceived to be, rather than what might be objectively regarded as, 'good information'. Such perceptions will in turn depend to a large extent on the other factors that can affect elected members' view of the local government world. Finance and the desire to provide a service for the public are pervasive issues for most, with Conservative members being more concerned about financial matters.

Further evidence (Usherwood 1993a) suggests that the advice of the professional officer is the most important specific influence on elected members. This is common across all the political parties. As Laffin and Young (1990) have observed, 'members find they often need a chief officer with whom they can discuss the specifics of front-line professional practice'.

It would appear that despite the new style of elected member cited in the literature (Boddy & Fudge; Gyford, 1985; Stewart 1988; et al. 1989) the well respected and well prepared chief librarian can still be an important influence on members' decisions.

The amount of influence perceived to be exerted by the officers is perhaps surprising at a time when, according to Stewart (1988), 'professionalism . . . is challenged politically, as councillors begin to question the validity of professional judgments'. However, there is at least some suggestion on the part of some members that, unlike some areas of local government, with the public library service it is, in the words of one politician, a 'case of letting the professionals get on with the job with encouragement and support' (Labour member, hung county council). With the exception of the high value placed on political ideology by members of the Labour Party there is little difference between the major factors that influence the members of the different parties. There are, however, some differences of emphasis.

Most local politicians serve on at least one other major committee in addition to the committee responsible for library services. Sadly for public librarians, the majority of members do not regard the library committee as the most important of their commitments. The role of the library committee is seen in terms of providing, protecting and promoting the service and the committee is perceived by its members as being held in low esteem by other members of the council. On the other hand, where library services are the responsibility of multifunction committees the data suggest that they are regarded as the most important topic for such committees. However, other research indicates that this is less likely to be the case where the library service is the responsibility of an education committee (Lomer & Rogers 1983). One might note in passing that this balance could be changed by the Conservative government's barely disguised aim to take schools out of local authority control.

The evidence would tend to suggest that, with perhaps the exception of hung councils, the committee is no longer the main forum for decision making. Some might argue that it never was. Be that as it may, decisions increasingly appear to be taken behind the closed doors of pre-agenda meetings and offices where the chief officer and chairperson discuss and debate the content of a report prior to its going to committee. That having been said, it is still true that 'committees dominate the working life of councillors and define their role within the local authority' (Rogers 1990). A significant number of members feel that, although reports to library committees are generally of a high quality, they tend to reflect the views of officers rather than those of members or of the public. Perhaps to counter this tendency, in many authorities before a report reaches the committee a draft is sent to the chairperson and/or a pre-agenda meeting for consideration.

Members expect the library committee to discuss financial and policy matters, staffing and any major changes to the service. A minority feels that 'everything' should be subject to committee discussion, whereas others consider that more could and should be left to the officers. This view was supported by a report from the Audit Commission (1990) which suggested that many councillors are wasting half their time discussing trivia at unnecessary meetings. More recently, the working party on the internal management of local authorities has produced an interesting report (*Community leadership and representation* 1993) illustrating ways in which local authorities can streamline their decision-making procedures while still maintaining effective community representation.

Despite the obvious frustrations, most local politicians currently find their work on the library committee satisfying. However, it remains to be seen whether that will be the case in the future as the power and influence of local government are reduced. Satisfaction is obtained as a result of getting things done for the library service, and/or in winning political battles. Labour and Liberal Democrat politicians in particular are frustrated by the lack of finance available for public library services, and by what they perceive to be the increasing loss of local autonomy. The introduction of party politics into library matters is found dissatisfying by about one in ten members. Others feel that library services have suffered in the past because of a lack of political impact.

A large majority of members regard the library committee as less party-political than most other committees of the councils they serve on. It is open to question whether this is a good thing for the public library service. In the past some professional librarians have valued the absence of politics in library matters, perhaps because features implemented on political grounds by one party may be rejected when another party comes to power, also on political grounds. Twenty-five years ago Budge (1971) said: 'Public libraries are popular. They should be free from political issues and library committees should be free from politics in their work'. A dozen years later Roger Stoakley (1983) put the argument even more strongly when he asked:

> What value have politics for us? Politics are all about conflict; one ideology against another. You never achieve anything worthwhile in this world through conflict. Conflict inevitably leads to alienation and alienation is certainly what we do not want in libraries.

In the eyes of some councillors, however, a lack of 'party politics' in library committees is linked to a lack of perceived importance. Members, said one, have 'bigger fish to fry elsewhere' (Conservative chairman, Outer London borough) and 'the library service only accounts for about 1% of the council's budget'. Thus one chairperson of a library committee has argued that:

> We've got to make our arguments for libraries and arts political ones. We've got to start to talk in language our colleagues will understand. For too long we've talked with pride about the absence of politics from the Libraries and Arts Committee (Nicholson 1987).

In addition, Professor John Stewart (1983) is of the opinion that: 'Local politics should be at the heart of library management. For politics bring change.'

In fact, party politics do play at least a small part in the operations of the majority of library committees and their importance, in some, has been perceived to have increased over recent years. In such a situation it is increasingly important that public librarians are politically aware, and that those with strategic management responsibilities develop skills that enable them to function effectively in the political arena. The implications of this, in terms of professional development and library education, are discussed in Chapter 11, which considers whether and how political astuteness and sensitivity can be taught and learnt.

The impact of politics also raises questions about the neutrality of the librarian and the related topic of political appointments. Research (Usherwood 1993a; Widdicombe Report 1986) tends to suggest that the danger of political appointments has probably been somewhat exaggerated (Baker 1984; Goodson-Wickes 1984). Although many Conservatives suggest that they are made by left-wing councils, Labour members argue strongly against the idea. This is not to say that there is not a relationship between an officer's politics and his or her appointment, but that it is more likely to be the result of the officer applying for a post in a particular authority than of any direct, crudely political intervention.

All things being equal, elected members want to appoint on merit, and are aware of the dangers of 'group think' (Janis 1968). Quite naturally, as in the private sector, organizations can be expected to appoint people who share their values and policy aims as these are the people most likely to deliver the service in an effective manner. This does not mean that there are not:

> . . . a few councils where . . . cowboys of the political world want to ride roughshod over the minority councillors and the paid administrators alike . . . and seek to appoint staff at senior level who share their views (Boynton 1986).

Such cowboys are not, however, just a modern phenomenon. Savage, as long ago as 1942, observed that: 'However able a librarian he won't be appointed by a Big Endian majority when he is known to be a Little Endian' (Savage 1942).

The data suggest that political allegiances do produce differences when it comes to elected members' opinions on some aspects of the public library service, notably on the use of volunteers, charging, contracting out and the provision of a premium service. However, given the views of an essentially right-wing central government of the time, it is interesting that, even among Conservative members, there is no overwhelming support for such ideas. For instance, whereas 47% of Conservative members agree or strongly agree with contracting out library services, 32% disagree or strongly disagree. In addition, only one of the four Conservative Chairpersons interviewed by Usherwood (1993a) was in favour of contracting out, and none supported the idea of a premium service as suggested in the Green Paper on *Financing our public library service*. Indeed, the figures suggest that the Conservative party at the local level is divided, or perhaps open-minded, on a number of the more contentious issues. For example, 31% of Conservatives agree or strongly agree that some aspects of the library service should be left to voluntary organizations, but 52% disagree or strongly disagree; 42% of the Conservative members agree or strongly agree with the idea of a premium service, but 53% disagree or strongly disagree. Research (Usherwood 1993a) has shown that, at a local level, most Conservatives pay little attention to ideology. This may be one reason for their rejection of some of the ideas emanating from the New Right.

Members of the other two parties appear to be less divided among themselves, or indeed with each other, on library issues. Thus, 100% of both Labour and Democrat members disagree or strongly disagree with the idea of contracting out library services, whereas 88% of Labour members and 84% of Democrat members disagree or strongly disagree with the idea of a premium service. The majority of members in all parties are against the introduction of charges for the loan of public library books, although there is stronger feeling against the idea among Labour and Democrat members.

In a study of the determinants of public policy, Sharpe and Newton (1984) asked, 'Does politics matter?' With regard to the management of the public library service the evidence suggests that it does, for a number of reasons. It matters in the very obvious sense of the local government review, education policy and other legislation and proposed legislation. It matters, perhaps above all, because librarians need to be aware of, and sensitive to, their local political environment.

Politicians of different persuasions do hold different views about the way the public library service should be financed and organized. That having been said, the majority of elected members serving on library committees have a real interest in the service and a concern for it. The vast majority have thought quite deeply about the library service and are generally supportive of it. In contrast to the view often expressed by professional librarians (Evans 1991; Gerard 1988; Jast 1935), many elected members do possess a reasonable knowledge of the scope and aims of the service. Their perception is, as it should be, different from that of the professional librarian. As domain theory (Kouses & Mico 1979) suggests, those operating in the policy domain and the management domain operate by different and contrasting principles. Likewise, Jones (1973), in discussing the functions and organization of councillors, argued that 'members and officials . . . are influenced by different pressures'.

Overall it is still possible to agree with Savage's (1942) perceptive remark that 'All parties (though not all men) seem to be in favour of libraries, at any rate in thriving and peaceful times'. However, in Britain's most recent and less than thriving times the demands emanating from the political realm have appeared to make some members less in favour of libraries. This is perhaps particularly true of those not serving on library committees.

The recent cutbacks in library services have led some to suggest that politicians undervalue the public library service (Cunningham 1991). Of course, it could also be argued that some professional librarians underestimate the importance of politics or the motivation of politicians. This is important because the way that 'different "actors" perceive and make sense of the world helps to explain organizational behaviour.' (Barrett & Fudge 1981). The data suggest that the different political actors 'make sense of the world' in different ways. Members of the Conservative party tend to be pragmatic in their approach, whereas Labour members are motivated by issues of social justice and the Liberal Democrats by community welfare. These differing perceptions and values would appear to make some difference in how members of the different political parties view the public library service. Sharpe and Newton (1984), in looking at the whole range of local government services, observed that:

> [Political] Parties . . . seem to provide crucial elements in the decision-making process. Perhaps the best analogy to a party in this context is that of a prism: the party transforms other major elements in line with party ideology and the need to get re-elected.

Although the evidence suggests that local politicians play an important part in the operation of public libraries, it is not suggested that a study of elected members or political parties can provide the best, or only, explanation of the decisions taken about library services. The management of public libraries, like that of any local government service, is a partnership between elected members and council employers. To quote from the 'Cheshire Values':

> Employees are responsible to councillors but they depend on each other for effectiveness. Mutual support within this partnership is necessary for the successful operation of the organization as a whole (Cheshire County Council nd.).

One might add that the successful operation of the organization as a whole also requires a mutual understanding of each group's aims and aspirations.

There is some anecdotal evidence to suggest that librarians' perceptions of local politicians may not always be entirely accurate. As a former library committee chairman has written:

> I asked [name of librarian] what he thought, and he said that some of his colleagues wouldn't know a politician from Father Christmas, and would be likely to ask for a present from either in exactly the same terms. I took this to mean that he had no great opinion of the political awareness of those he had in mind (Monroe 1987).

In his memoirs David Gerard (1988), who was among other things City Librarian of Nottingham, confesses that, 'Generally the world of elected members was inscrutable to me'. It is to be hoped that this is not the case with today's generation of public librarians. Management in the public sector has to be concerned with the stuff of politics. It is this rather than the market or theories of economic production that should be of major interest to today's public library managers. To quote Ranson and Stewart (1994), 'The task of management in the public domain is to enable political judgment'.

Chapter 3

Structures, strategies, technology and the management of change

THE LOCAL GOVERNMENT review was, in every sense of the term, the result of political judgment. It has also been a major concern for many public library managers. For a long time the results of this tortuous and unhappy affair, which was set in train by the 1992 Local Government Act, were in doubt. The uncertainty was increased when 'the Environment Secretary . . . effectively sacked the . . . chairman of the Local Government Commission' (Simmons 1995). Within the library profession the review provoked considerable debate about the optimum size for a public library authority. Research carried out by Midwinter and McVicar (1993,1994) tended to suggest that larger authorities produced economies of scale. The Library Association (1994a), although not hostile to change as such, also concluded that the larger county authorities provided a more cost-effective service and mounted a campaign that received the support of notable people from literature, the arts and entertainment (Cleese and others 1994).

It is now clear that the result of the review will be a larger number of smaller authorities. The Library Association has estimated that by April 1998 there will be 208 public library authorities in the United Kingdom. This represents a considerable increase on the 167 that existed prior to the review, and has significant implications for the management of the service.

Some in the profession argued that the local government review was political and had more to do with Conservative political ambitions than good management. Indeed, many feared that the result would be a worse rather than a better library service. Hopkins (1994), for instance, was particularly concerned about the implications for central support services and the library supply industry. Others feared the difficulties that would result from splitting up centralized resources, and suggested that there would be problems in maintaining specialist services such as rural mobiles and programmes for minority ethnic communities.

The review has also provided a new dimension to the debate over the most appropriate place for the public library in the local authority structure. Asked, as part of the present research, what he or she considered the most significant change in public library management in the past five years, one respondent observed:

> The position of public libraries within the overall structure in individual local authorities often determines the main element of change. It is evident that public librarians have less and less access directly to the top level of management. (English metropolitan district)

Another respondent had noticed:

> . . . an erosion of the basics of public libraries that have become even greater Cinderella services. This erosion is reflected in:
> (a) heads of library services becoming third tier;
> (b) libraries being subsumed into mega directorates;
> (c) loss of library committees;
> (d) library staff pay falling behind comparable public and private sector occupations. (London Borough)

Evidence in support of the last point was provided by the case of the county council that advertised a head of libraries, museums and archives post at a totally inadequate salary, and also proposed to appoint a county librarian at a level beneath the head of service. The county council concerned argued that the lower salary was justified as, under the local government review one of its major towns was to become a unitary authority.

In Wales, where the new local authorities are now in place, autonomous library departments have virtually disappeared and the majority of library services have been absorbed into education- or leisure-based directorates. There is some concern that when all the new and smaller unitary authorities come into operation more library services will be linked with leisure or education departments, and consequently lose out in terms of finance and political influence. As one respondent observed, in somewhat staccato fashion:

> Libraries absorbed into leisure departments. Funding reduced while leisure funding increased. Routes of consultation with members removed. (Scottish District)

Of course there is nothing new in such connections. For many years county libraries were part of education departments, and over 20 years ago it was being claimed that 'the fundamental objectives of the library service can be closely related to those of *all* recreational services' (Tirisias 1975, emphasis added). One respondent argued that in the present situation, with the move 'towards large multidiscplinary departments, in order to keep your 'profile' managers [should] get involved in many other areas apart from the library service.' (English metropolitan district)

The advantages and disadvantages of mega directorates for libraries are well known and we need only briefly repeat them here. Those who argue in favour of such arrangements suggest that libraries will benefit from a larger budget, and will have the opportunity to employ specialists that could not be justified in smaller departments. They also argue that, as larger departments, the directorates will have greater political attraction for elected members, that they provide opportunities for staff to develop interdisciplinary skills and provide high flyers with greater managerial opportunities.

Those who argue for separate library departments would point to the possible downgrading of library services and library officers in the large directorates. They would also refer to the problems faced by a chief librarian when he or she does not have easy access to politicians and chief officers. One respondent to the present study stated that already:

> Many of the major decisions affecting public library services are made by people not in the profession, e.g. directors of leisure and recreation departments which include libraries. Chief librarians are often *not* chief officers and *not* on the management team of their authorities. (Scottish District, original emphasis)

Others fear that different services might be financed at the public library's expense. They also point to the commercial culture of the leisure world, which could prove dangerous for public libraries in the present political climate. Such arguments have been further strengthened by recent developments which mean that since 1988 local authorities have had to submit some sport and leisure facilities to competitive tendering. It is perhaps not a coincidence that the man who encouraged 'Brent [to] enthusiastically put up two of its branch libraries . . . is not a professional librarian. His background is in arts and leisure administration' (Walker, D. 1994).

Recent advertisements for directors in a number of authorities suggest, however, that the multidisciplinary trend is likely to increase. There is evidence to show that more and more authorities are moving towards a smaller executive group of chief officers. A recent report (*Portrait of change* 1996) indicates that the average top management team has lost one officer since 1989, whereas the number of committees has fallen by nearly two over the same period. In Wales, 'dilution and demotion seem to be the general fate of public libraries . . . But some librarians have come out pretty well. The new (mostly smaller) authorities are streamlining their structure' (Welsh Reorganization 1996).

In the words of one respondent, 'the incorporation of library services into bigger corporate departments has had advantages as well as disadvantages'. Given that, whether we like it or not, this is likely to be the pattern for the future, it seems we should seek a more logical arrangement than many of those currently on offer. The author and others (Arnold & Usherwood 1976; Corbett 1979; Usherwood 1979) have long questioned the logic of the connection with leisure. More recently, Law (1996) has commented on its limiting effect, observing that:

> Public libraries have been sucked into the morass of local government reforms and placed in leisure groupings. There they have sat, comfortably meeting user needs rather than creating user aspirations.

The education option would also seem to reduce the potential of the public library service in the information age. There is also the fact that the library can be a very small fish in the large education pool. That having been said, there are some who argue that if the present government continues to take the education function away from local councils, the library service could become a more important part of an education department.

The author would argue for a solution that would place the public library within a more logical group of services. It is a structure that will encourage the ambitious librarian to involve him or herself in the general work of the local authority, and provide opportunities for promotion to higher managerial positions. It will, in the words of one our respondents, permit librarians to take advantage of 'the new perspectives and opportunities [multidisciplinary departments] can bring' (English County). As such it will leave the management option open, but also enable the librarian's professional skills to be more fully put to use for the benefit of the local authority and the local community. In addition, it is a structure in which librarians will find greater professional and personal satisfaction. It is this professional satisfaction that many, but admittedly not all, librarians find lacking in some of the current and proposed structural arrangements.

The structure would be based on a directorate concerned with the acquisition, organization and communication of information, ideas and works of imagination. As such it would include part of a local authority's recreation function and parts of the education function and arts and cultural activities. It is suggested that the public library should become an integral part of a directorate or department of communications. The precise name is less important than the function, but we believe that such directorates should be responsible for libraries, archives and museums, arts provision, IT and other council-wide information services, and perhaps some aspects of press and publications.

All the areas included in the suggested 'communications' department are linked with the underlying purpose of the public library. Such an arrangement would not only do away with some of the illogical and wasteful combinations that exist at the moment (bibliographies and baths, for example), but would also strengthen librarians' logical and rightful links with other areas such as information technology, one-stop information services and the like. Readers will be only too aware of library services that have never had, or have lost control of the civic information role to another town hall department.

As Worrall (1995) has indicated, a combination of the revised local government structures, new information technologies and developments such as the Citizen's Charter means that local authorities will have to:

> . . . think more creatively about how information should be managed, how it should be used to enhance the role and positioning of local government in the community, and how it could be used to improve the quality of policy making and service delivery.

At the same time there must be mechanisms not just to manage the information but to provide public access to it. This surely is a strategic role for the public library service, but there are some doubts that it is one for which the profession is fully prepared.

Noting what he calls 'honourable exceptions', Law (1996) asks, 'where on earth have been the UK equivalents of the pioneers of Pike's Peak in Colorado who developed Maggie's Place a decade ago? Or where are the champions of the Freenet movement?' Information provision has become a role for planners, corporate planners and the rest. There is little logic in a situation where public librarians are having less to do with one of their basic functions (the organization and dissemination of information) yet more to do with activities at best only distantly related to their professional skills. The story of the librarian responsible for a crematorium is not apocryphal.

Within library services there have also been changes in management structures. According to one respondent to our present study:

> The most significant change in library management over the last five years is the reduction of the hierarchy with flattened structures, removal of layers etc. (English metropolitan district)

As Figure 3.1 shows, this has been widely welcomed by public library managers.

Management structure roles and processes are also being changed by technological developments. The technology can provide management information systems and therefore support many management activities. New technologies have the power not only to change the kind of services that public libraries provide but also to change the way in which those services are managed and decisions are taken. In some cases this may change the shape of the library organization. It can also lead to a disintegration of established hierarchies.

IT is already being used to enable new processes. Newish developments such as business process re-engineering (BPR) reflect attempts to break away from old rules, regulations and basic assumptions that underlie how a public library is organized. Such technological development can alter the distribution of power in

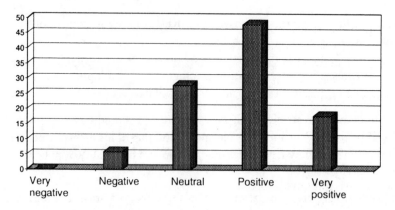

Fig. 3.1 *Attitude to reduction in management layers*

the library as the content of specific jobs is affected. The technology can give power to IT specialists who possess 'expert power', while at the same time taking power away from those who may have traditionally held it. Thus power may shift, or be perceived to shift, in favour of the computer experts and away from (say) cataloguers or community librarians. In the changing situation brought about by the introduction of new technology the relative importance of different occupations is likely to change. Indeed, data obtained for this study suggest that some chief librarians may also suffer the problems associated with loss of status and a reduced sense of personal worth.

Electronic communication can also alter the ways in which ideas are communicated and understood within organizations. Writers have observed 'unfavourable changes in which social aspects such as face to face relationships are replaced with impersonal communication through the use of computer mediated communication' (Baskerville & Smithson 1995). At the same time, it is argued that facilities such as groupware and e-mail can benefit teamwork and help facilitate organizational change.

It is now common in the literature to see IT referred to as a strategic resource that requires particular management skills. Many staff will require training to use the new technology effectively. In particular, great attention needs to be paid to the interaction between library staff and the new technology because it is unrealistic to expect that this degree of change, be it for good or bad, can take place without a significant level of individual and organizational disturbance.

Library managers will need to be sensitive in dealing with this situation. There is a danger that an obsession with IT will cause problems unless correct emphasis is placed on the needs of people. Too many of those involved with managing the new technologies have ignored the human dimension. Human beings are more complicated than machines, and solving human problems often requires more than technical solutions. In this context we need to be aware of the impact of IT, on public library services and the people who work in them.

In a recent study, Heaton and Brown (1995), found that staff are experiencing increased stress as a result of working at computer terminals, and because of expectations of increased productivity when technology is introduced into libraries. The public library manager will then have to develop skills that will enable him or her to help others cope with the new technologies, adapt to new practices and cope with the uncertainties of technological change. Uncertainty occurs when people lack information about future events and are unable to predict alternative solutions and outcomes. Managers in the public library service will need to develop means and strategies and personnel to deal with uncertainty. In any organization those who are able to undertake this task will be among the most powerful.

The good public library manager will anticipate the human factors associated with change, and appreciate that staff will be concerned about their future. They will, for instance, want to know if the new technology will create extra jobs or reduce the number available. For many IT is still perceived as a threat and a cause for economic concern. This is not surprising when one reads, in a paper intended to encourage BPR, statements such as:

> IT . . . underpins business re-engineering by streamlining processes so that, for example, one person can do the same work that previously would have involved several people in different departments (CCTA 1994).

This is taken from a document published by the Government Centre for Information Systems. With this kind of admission coming from official sources it is not surprising that people sometimes wonder if they will still have a job when the technology finally arrives.

Technology can both enrich and dehumanize and deskill library work. The professional jury is still out on the degree to which each is true. Reuter (1991) found that librarians did not consider themselves deskilled. However, Harris (1992) is of the opinion that 'on balance, librarianship is being deskilled and deprofessionalized, at least with respect to its traditional functions'. This may be of some benefit to paraprofessionals. Goulding (1996) found that the new technology 'can make assistants' work more varied and interesting . . . As librarians acquire more . . . pieces of technological equipment staff have to learn to use them and exploit what they offer to the full. As a result the range of tasks and complexity of the assistant's job has increased.'

On the other hand, it is likely that some hard-earned skills will become less useful. IT may reduce the value of some previous training and experience. The theoretical knowledge of the younger, and perhaps better educated (in IT terms), staff may become more important than the experience of the older member of staff. However, if we simply accept the erosion of professional skills we may well be creating problems for the future. We will, at the very least, be reducing the capabilities of future librarians. We may not yet have turned library professionals into button-pushing robots, but it will not be in the professional or public interest to reduce the members of a personal service profession (Halmos 1970) to mere automata.

The computer's memory can be more easily erased than that of the individual. Human beings have the problem of not forgetting. John Smith, the former county librarian of Cumbria, gives an example of this. He told a professional conference :

> I can remember five years after introducing a computer catalogue, finding a fully maintained, hand written card catalogue at one of my branches (Smith 1982).

Staff may find what they know already interfering with what they need to know.

Research such as that carried out by Rogers (1962) has shown that people differ in their readiness to accept change. Briefly, he indicated that people fall into five different types:

- innovators
- early adapters
- the early majority
- the late majority
- laggards.

Work carried out at the then Polytechnic of the South Bank found that:

> Certain types of people resist change more than others. Those that have worked for the library for a longer period of time are more resistant to change because they have more time and money vested in the status quo. Those that have been here for a shorter period of time are more amenable to change since they have no strong commitment to the old . . . system and are more adaptable to new situations.

For some of the older staff change can be perceived as an indictment of the old way of doing things (Kanter 1985). It is also the case that people vary according to the nature of the change. For instance, some may find it easier to deal with some aspects of social change than with technological change, and vice versa.

A mini industry has developed in advising library managers and others how to deal with change (see, for example, Underwood 1990, Kanter 1983, 1985) and there is no need to revisit all their ideas here. Suffice it to say that the process is not orderly, and it may take many months for people to adjust to and adopt new ideas and methods of working. Those responsible for managing change need to take this into account. Significant interpersonal skills are required to undertake the coaching, counselling and confidence building that is required. Managers need to empathize to ensure that staff 'get over' a major imposed change without personal or organizational damage.

Recently, Cleveland Council used bereavement counsellors to help their staff deal with what was, for them, the particularly traumatic change of local government reorganization. This is an interesting development and reflects the fact that people exposed to an imposed change take time to adjust because they often experience loss. The process is summarized as follows:

- Stage 1:   Shock; shut down thinking;
- Stage 2:   Resistance; anger; anxiety; refusal to let go;
- Stage 3:   Acknowledgement; letting go; grief and sadness;
- Stage 4:   Adaptation; change.

Of course, not all resistance to change is necessarily bad. Indeed such resistance may sometimes be useful. Individuals and organizations need periods of stability to take stock and assimilate the changes that have already taken place in their organizational world. Toffler made much the same kind of point when he argued that we need stability zones so that we can deal with the change happening around us.

Indeed, it is a major argument of the present text that many of the changes imposed on the public library service in the last decade have not been beneficial for the service, the people who use it or the people who manage it. The management writer J. B. Harvey (1988) has written about the management of agreement, and there is plenty of evidence to suggest that some involved in the management of public services have simply taken the line of least resistance and gone along with the conventional wisdoms as espoused by the gurus of the new managerialism.

The new technology itself may be one cause of this. There is the danger of what has been called 'nuggetizing' [whereby] 'information is packaged, the more easily accessible the package the better. The result is a kind of brittle world in which all room for doubt, debate, speculation and analysis is displaced by simple statement nuggets' (Brown, 1995). For good decisions to be made managers must have the ability to transform information into intelligence.

It has also been argued that the new technology has made it more difficult for politicians in that elected 'members' ability to encompass the range of the technology related aspects of librarianship and information work has diminished' (Kinnell 1996). Public libraries will therefore require staff and politicians who can recognize the threats and opportunities of change. In the context of IT this means staff who have the ability to make sound investment decisions and to use information technology for the benefit of the public.

Information technology provides us with many new opportunities to pursue the public library ideal of service to the community, but this is unlikely to be achieved unless there is a degree of regulation and/or substantial public investment. In an area as important as the communication of information and ideas, regulations will be needed to protect and provide for the information-poor. This, of course, is to argue against the current fashion for the deregulation of everything.

The Labour Party says that, if elected, it will 'insist that the providers of the networks lay a two-way broadband feed into every public library, every school, every health centre, every hospital and every Citizen's Advice Bureau' (Labour Party 1995). The recent DNH Public Library Review also recommended that 'the principle of free and equal access to library materials should be extended when conditions allow', and makes

> . . . a case for allowing uncharged access to those Internet or World Wide Web sources that are essentially 'free', that is, available at no more than the cost of local calls to telecommunications modes (Aslib 1995).

This in fact should be a minimum requirement at a time when success is often linked with the ability to use computers and access the superhighways of the information world.

Unless there is universal access there is a very real danger that the gap will widen between the rich and the poor, the educated and the uneducated, the black and the white. As Frankena and Frankena (1986) have observed, technical expertise has become 'a crucial political resource in controversies, because access to knowledge and the resulting ability to question the data and information used to legitimate decisions is an essential basis for power and influence'. The public library could be an important agency to help people acquire such technical expertise and gain confidence in the use of new technology.

Anybody can visit and make use of a public library, but it is highly unlikely that electronic newspapers and expensive electronic equipment will be widely available in the slum houses of the inner city or the cardboard homes of the dispossessed thrown on to the streets by political processes that they don't understand. The public library could help to reduce such inequality by becoming an integral part of an information infrastructure, taking the information superhighway to rural lanes and the crowded back streets of the inner city.

This will not happen if the development of IT is left to commercial and market forces alone. However, the present (1996) British government is so ideologically blinkered that it maintains, and indeed seeks to persuade the world, that 'only businesses can provide the investment and enterprise to build the superhighway that will form the global information society' (Taylor 1996).

In contrast, the Danish government has recognized the contribution that can be made by public library and information services. In its consideration of the *Info Society 2000* it states as Policy 17 that:

> Even in the future – when electronic publications will be taking over the role of magazines and books – libraries must maintain a major intermediary function as providers of public information to all citizens and must help the public to navigate through the increasing flood of information (From Vision to Action 1995).

If the public library service is to be an agent to produce informed citizens, it will need to provide effective and equal access to words, images and sound.

Peter Young, the Executive Director of the US National Commission on Libraries and Information Science (NCLIS), has said that 'libraries provide more than computers, conduits and content: libraries provide the context for answering questions and navigating the Internet and the intellectual output of the human race. Interactive networks change political economic and social processes' (Tullis 1995).

There is also the question of the impact of information technology on our patterns of social interaction, indeed on the very nature of the communities in which we live and work. 'Technology', wrote the playwright Max Frisch, is 'the knack of so arranging the world that we don't have to experience it'. Along with Frisch, the author believes that the virtual world provides a far more shallow range of experiences than that provided by the real world of living people. However, if the futurologists are correct and people are to work in front of VDUs and computer consoles, and children are to be educated in the same way, and infotainment is to be provided down a cable or phone line, we have to consider what will be the future for community services such as schools and libraries?

The publicity for a recent American conference asked: 'as publishers identify their electronic information markets will they progressively employ expert systems and other artificial intelligence systems to replace the reference activity of the local library, thereby substituting self-service for mediated service?' (Newhard 1993). Similar questions are being asked, and in their own terms answered, by the Right in this country. For example:

> The notion that the Adam Smith Institute takes is that modern technology makes it increasingly easier to have service output tailor-made to individual needs instead of us all having to take a standard product. (Pirie, quoted in Gosling 1993)

On the other hand, public library-oriented Freenets can be used by a wide range of social groups. In Seattle, for instance, a group of homeless men 'discovered the

Internet . . . and are now considered to be the in-house experts on the information highway' (Jordan 1994). Maryland opened its first cyberlibrary by allowing its citizens a free connection to the Internet. This project, known as Sailor, uses the resources of public, school and academic libraries throughout the state. It has provoked a great deal of discussion, not the least of which is on the Net itself. In the end, what it does, to quote Powledge (1994), is to fuse 'Internet customers with an equally vigorous but much older tradition of free information – that of the public library'.

In any organization change is an inevitable process but, as the above indicates, in embracing the new we can sometimes rediscover our original purpose. The understandable desire for progress and improvement must be allowed to flourish, but in a less corrosive manner than that of the recent past. As we have seen, legislative changes such as the local government review, the new technology and structures have all been forces for change. It is, however, not necessary to be against change per se to argue that not all change is good, and that not all resistance to change is bad.

Change can sometimes be a false comforter. As Washington Irving (1824) realized :

> There is a certain relief in change even though it be from bad to worse. As I have found travelling in a stage coach, that it is often a comfort to shift one's position and be bruised in a new place.

The gurus tell us that resistance to change is not always because of the change itself, but because people have to adjust themselves to change. They may also have fears of the kind discussed earlier. Of course there will be times when library managers will want and need their staff to accept the challenge of change. Equally we must not be tempted to change simply for changes' sake. Those who resist or question may sometimes have a legitimate point of view.

Part 2

Professional qualities?

Conservative governments justified incursions into producer power by using a rhetoric of improving quality in the interests of the 'sovereign consumer'. What this implied was a fundamental challenge to the legitimacy and working practices of professionals and other occupational groups within the public sector. IAN KIRKPATRICK and MIGUEL LUCIO,
The politics of quality in the public sector, 1995

Chapter 4

Quality qualified

J UDGING BY THE quantity of the literature alone, quality management is a private sector idea that is now much in vogue in the management of public services. However, experienced public library managers could be forgiven if they sometimes wonder what all the fuss is about. The idea that success, in either business or service, depends on the 'quality' of the product or output is not new. As speakers at a recent international symposium (Kanji 1995) sought to demonstrate, total quality management (TQM) is not a new idea: several at that meeting traced it back to historical sources, the earliest being Aristotle in his *Metaphysics*. From a more practical perspective, anyone who has checked either their own work or someone else's for mistakes, has been a 'quality manager'.

That having been said, 'quality' has become the new buzzword in the literature and practice of management. It is a concept that is now debated in both the public and the private sectors, and is supported by the main political parties. In Britain the Conservatives' Citizen's Charter (1991) emphasizes the importance of quality in local authority services, while the Labour Party seeks 'to ensure that quality is the hallmark of all local services' (Labour Party 1991).

However, despite the wide use of the term, 'there is no consensus about the meaning of quality' (Pfeffer & Coote 1991) and academics and practitioners alike are attempting to answer the question what is meant by 'quality'? (Sanderson 1992).

There are some definitions with which readers will be familiar. For example, British Standard BS4778 (BSI 1987) defines quality as 'the totality of features and characteristics of a product or service that bear on its ability to satisfy stated or implied needs'. Juran (1979) defines it more simply as: 'fitness for purpose or use'. Stewart and Walsh (1989), who write specifically about public services, define a quality service as one that: 'does what it is intended to do and is responsive to the needs of the user'.

Although these definitions seem relatively clear, they are not particularly helpful to the manager of a public service. First, they beg the question, What does 'quality' mean in the context of a particular product or service? For instance a manager specifying the requirements for a high-quality database would come up with a list of attributes very different from those of a manager trying to define a 'quality' counter service at a community library.

Secondly, most of the definitions approach quality in terms of the end product. Of course, in many respects this is perfectly legitimate since the outcome of any effort to improve quality must be a better product or service, measured by increased user satisfaction. However, differences in approach to quality are revealed when the question is asked, How might the quality of this service or product best be raised? The answers may not only involve adjustments to the end product or service, to improve its performance, but also include the application of specific techniques to improve the efficiency of processes within the organization. This might involve a review of organizational relationships, or indeed a fundamental rethink of how the organization approaches its purpose.

The literature and management practice demonstrate many different approaches to the concept of quality. Writers (Foster & Whittle 1989) have referred to the 'quality management maze' and although phrases such as 'quality centre', 'quality assurance' and 'total quality management' are sometimes used interchangeably, they actually reflect very different views of the subject. It has been argued, for instance, that public service managers need to be able to differentiate between 'quality that derives from systems [and] quality that derives from people and their commitment' (Walsh 1992). Similarly, recent research (Milner et al. in press) has thrown considerable doubt on the practical application of BS5750/ISO9000 to services such as public libraries, that deal with information, imagination and ideas, rather than a physical product. These approaches to quality, with their emphasis on job design and a managerial bureaucracy, have much in common with scientific management and the Taylorian ethos. Indeed, as has been mentioned earlier, a number of writers (see, for example, Pollitt 1993) believe that Taylorism is very much part of the new managerialism.

Pfeffer and Coote (1991) have identified a number of different approaches to quality, but argue that many fail in terms of public service management 'because they do not acknowledge important distinctions between commerce and welfare'. The approaches identified by Pfeffer and Coote are as follows:

1   The traditional approach. This is associated with very high standards of production, delivery and presentation, the kind of quality that goes with the no-expense-spared approach of expensive restaurants, French fragrances, Rolls Royce cars and beautifully bound books.

2   The scientific approach. This is seen in those organizations that have focused on performance indicators. It is the approach to quality advocated in *Keys to success* (Office of Arts and Libraries 1990 and *The Citizen's Charter performance indicators* (Audit Commission 1992).

3 The managerial or excellence approach. This can be found in the work of Peters and Waterman (1982). The aim is customer satisfaction and the writers assume that quality is achieved by constantly striving to meet customer requirements.

4 The consumerist approach. This seeks to put power in the hands of the consumer by giving her or him redress for complaints.

5 The democratic approach. This has been developed by Pfeffer and Coote as a reaction against some of the approaches given above. It seeks to satisfy the community as a whole and to achieve common goals, and they would argue that it is the most appropriate model for public services.

Pfeffer and Coote's research is significant in that it indicates that a different perspective may be necessary for public sector organizations. Their work concentrates not only on what defines the quality of a service, but also on who should define that quality. These are important matters that will be considered later.

The literature of quality management in the profession is voluminous, and is growing (Milner et al 1994). The variety of approaches it reveals shows that for libraries the quality maze has not yet been solved. Moreover, it has been established that many library authorities are undertaking activities which contribute to a quality service, although this term is sometimes not used. Evidence of this can be found in the research carried out by Porter (1992) into quality initiatives in British library and information services, Kinnell and MacDougall's (1993) work on marketing, and Levy and Usherwood's (1992) project on interpersonal skills, and the joint research recently undertaken by Sheffield and Loughborough universities (Milner et al. in press).

The emphasis on quality management has been accelerated by a number of factors, including the government's expectation that public services will adopt a business ethos, and the financial constraints that have been imposed on those services. There was also for some time a pressure to gain certification to quality standards such as BS 5750 and ISO 9000. In addition, performance indicators are increasingly being used as tools to enhance the quality of service delivery (Sumsion 1993). Alongside this there is what Walsh (1992) has called the maturity of public service. The emphasis has now moved from *more* housing, *more* education, *more* health care etc. to *better* housing, *better* education and *better* health care.

Other writers, notably Kirkpatrick and Lucio (1995), have identified a more overt political agenda. They argue that 'quality' has been used to increase the managerial control of professionals and to legitimate changes in work practices, terms and conditions in organizations. Interestingly, they use the library profession as part of their argument. Their recent collection includes a paper which shows 'the development of performance indicators . . . steadily eroding the traditional role of professional librarians' (Davies & Kirkpatrick 1995). A respondent to the survey carried out for this book also linked quality with the political agenda. He said, 'I see quality programmes as part of the strategy to privatize libraries' (London borough).

It is certainly true that competitive tendering, compulsory or otherwise, has also been part of the government's approach to local government. Whatever one might feel about this process, it has led to an increased concern for service specifications. The new emphasis on contracts in local government means that it has become increasingly important to establish definitive approaches to quality as a prelude to the tendering process.

In a very real way this reflects our different expectations of the motivations of the public and private sectors. As Flynn (1993) observes:

> If it is the case that service providers are motivated by a desire to provide a good service, is specifying the service in such a way that it can be bought and sold (the commodification of service) desirable?

On the whole we have trusted public service and professional library staff to do their best and not to act in a dishonest way. Public services have been built on trust relationships, which are less often to be found in the free market. Once the service is to be contracted out to different organizations with different sets of values and priorities, experience has shown that we need a very detailed specification of what they intend to do and an equally detailed account of what they have done.

As Figure 4.1 shows, 77% of those responding to the present study felt that the movement towards quality management had been a significant force for change over the past five years.

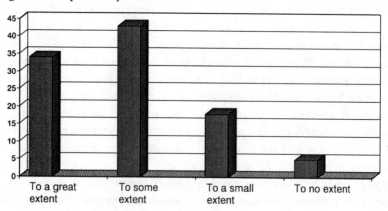

Fig. 4.1 *Quality management as a reason for change*

In an attempt to discover the extent to which quality initiatives had been adopted in public libraries, researchers at Sheffield and Loughborough universities asked the following questions of library managers:

1   What approaches to quality have been adopted by the library service? (e.g. Never ending improvement; BS5750; Total quality environment; TQM etc.)

2   Why has the quality concept been introduced by the library service and how has the concept affected the determination of performance indicators?

3   What quality systems are perceived to be in place? That is, systems for collecting, measuring and using information in order to support decision making.

4   Why were these approaches adopted?

5   What organizational structures have been introduced to enhance the delivery of quality services?

6   What are the attitudes of staff to 'quality management'? Porter (1992) emphasizes the importance of ascertaining the attitudes of middle management and frontline staff.

7   What organizational commitment is evident with regard to staff development for quality management?

8   How does the library organization 'get close to the customer'?

9   What is the role of elected members in the quality management of the service and how is this developed?

10   How has QM been evaluated and how does it relate to the library's stated objectives/mission statement/charter?

11   What has been the impact of 'quality management' on the delivery of the library service?

12   In the opinion of elected members and officers does 'quality management' work?

A questionnaire was sent to every public library authority in the UK and achieved an 81% response rate. The data therefore provide a fairly accurate picture of the current state of play with regard to quality in the public library sector. One of the more interesting findings is that, despite the amount of literature about the subject and its perceived importance, 62% of authorities responding said that they did not have a quality programme in place; 19% did claim to have such a programme and the remaining 19% were in the process of establishing one.

This may suggest that those who argue that more rhetoric than reality is associated with the concept of quality management may have a valid point. Haigh and Morris (1995) among others have asked:

What is the practising manager, seeking to embark upon a corporate quality initiative, to make of this plethora of knowledge and advocacy? All too frequently it would appear to be that the answer can be encapsulated in three little words: 'not a lot'.

Moreover, when asked if they had any specific quality initiative, 47% of respondents indicated that their service did not. Among the rest the greatest interest is in Investors in People (26.5%) and the Charter mark (18.5%). There is a 13.5% adoption rate for customer contracts, 10% for TQM and 10% for quality circles. Only 3.5% claimed to have adopted BS5750/ ISO9000: support here for Bajaria's (1995) view that ISO 9000 is 'a self inflicted human misery . . . making bad things in a certified way'.

When asked about the criteria used to measure the quality of the services delivered, respondents to the Loughborough/Sheffield study indicated that they used the following measures:

- 89% used existing performance indicators;
- 65% indicated that they used complaints;
- 49% measured success against predetermined targets;
- 49% used compliments;
- 35% took account of greater value for money;
- 25% used customer satisfaction surveys.

Other measures mentioned included comparisons with other library services, the number of books issued and the perceptions of elected members.

Librarians completing the Sheffield/Loughborough questionnaire were also asked to give their views on what they thought were the three most important quality features of a public library service. Although a great many features were cited, there was some degree of consensus in the response.

- 62% highlighted the importance of having skilled, courteous employees;
- 57% stressed the importance of an appropriate range and quality of resources;
- 32% stated that a welcoming environment was important.

Respondents were also asked to indicate those areas they felt needed the greatest improvement in their own service. Apart from one authority that felt no need to do anything, the priorities for improvement were as follows:

- Employees involved in contact with clients should have the knowledge to answer questions or make appropriate referrals.
- Opening hours should be convenient for the majority of clients.
- Clear guiding is necessary to enable clients to find their way around the library.
- A good book stock is essential.

• Libraries must make clients aware of the standards of service they can expect.

As indicated earlier, differences of approach to the issue of quality are reflected in the way people respond to the question, What defines the quality of the service? As Walsh (1995) has argued:

It is perfectly possible for one person to see a service as being of high quality and another to see it as of poor quality, with both citing precisely the same criteria in support of their arguments. The market has always had difficulty dealing with the issue of quality, especially in the case of complex services.

From a different perspective the Audit Commission (1993) proposes that quality management should focus on four key areas:

1 Quality of communication. Does the council (in this case the library service) communicate with, and listen to and understand, users?

2 Quality of specification. Is this understanding converted into clear standards for service delivery?

3 Quality of delivery. Are the standards actually delivered, and is remedial action taken when failure occurs?

4 Quality of people. Are staff motivated, trained, well managed and supported by quality systems?

Developing the final point, the research at Sheffield and Loughborough sought to ascertain what systems were in place in public libraries, and the use made of them. For instance, how should a library service deal with complaints? Should complainants be treated as a valuable asset? To what level should authority to deal with them be delegated?

In responding to the Sheffield/Loughborough research instrument, many librarians tended to reflect the fashionable ideas to be found in the works of the quality gurus. Thus empowerment was talked about a great deal, but appeared to be practised rather less. Indeed, respondents sometimes seemed uncertain as to how they could, or even if they wanted to, develop a culture that 'empowers'. In a seminar held two-thirds of the way through the project they raised a number of questions, for instance: Does everybody necessarily want to be empowered? What benefits can be gained and what are the dangers of empowerment? Further work in this area is clearly required and the relationship between quality initiatives and staff motivation is currently the subject of a doctoral study at Sheffield (Mistry & Usherwood 1995).

The Sheffield/Loughborough joint project, in common with the DNH public library review, also raised questions about leadership. These and similar studies, provide a considerable body of evidence to suggest that in the public library sector we need to identify and consider the leadership skills and personal attributes that are essential for success. What are the barriers to success, and what is the difference between a leader and a manager? These are issues that are considered further in Chapter 10.

Several of the drawbacks associated with the implementation of QM highlighted in responses referred to the need to put even greater time and effort into managing the service. In particular, skills seemed to be lacking in managing meetings, in team working and in communication with employees. Particularly emphasized was the lack of adequate opportunity for successful and meaningful upward communication.

In its approach to staff, the concept of total quality management appears, on one level, to have much in common with the Y end of Mcgregor's X – Y continuum (McGregor 1960). However, respondents to the Sheffield/Loughborough study seemed unsure as to how far it was necessary to involve employees working with QM: for instance, there was no clear consensus about who needed to know and understand 'the tools of the system'. Some felt that it was a matter for everyone, whereas others would leave it to a select few. This is perhaps a reflection of a larger problem suggested earlier. The present paradox is that whereas effective QM requires managers to have faith in their workers it is being practised in a national political climate that distrusts workers and in many ways reflects the ideas of Taylorism.

It is difficult to see how these two philosophies can successfully coexist. Deming (1986), in a much quoted phrase has said that companies 'must drive out fear so that everyone may work effectively'. However, as we have seen, there is currently much fear among the staff of public libraries. Experience elsewhere has also indicated that 'TQM does not readily blend with wave after wave of restructuring, downsizing and re-engineering.' (*The straining of quality* 1995).

Cost is an ever-present factor in the public library service, and despite some of the claims of the private sector gurus who 'insist that "quality is free" it is hard to see, how, in the public services, this could *always* be so (unless either "quality" or "free" are very idiosyncratically defined)' (Pollitt 1993, original emphasis).

The primacy of the user has long been recognized by the library profession and, as Figure 4.2 indicates, the vast majority (97%) of respondents to the present study felt that the focus on user needs had increased in the past five years.

However, this should not be confused with the 'focus on the customer' idea which is so prevalent in the quality literature. It is an issue that is more fully debated in later chapters, but suffice it to say that it causes one to revisit the familiar question as to who should define the quality of the public library service.

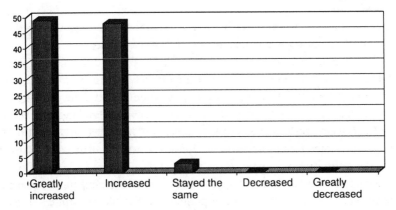

Fig. 4.2 *Focus on user needs*

There are at least three possibilities:

1 A department, organization, or agency external to the organization. Since a library or information unit is likely to be part of a larger organization, it is common for the quality agenda to be set by someone outside the unit. This may, of course, be the parent organization to which the library or information service belongs. A commercial company might seek BS 5750/ISO 9000 accreditation, to secure wider markets. The information unit serving the company would, in that instance, have no choice but to adopt the approach, irrespective of its own specific needs.

For public services there are also political considerations. In the UK the Audit Commission has established comparative performance indicators for local authorities, and the Prime Minister's office has launched the Citizen's Charter (1991) initiative. The Prime Minister has stressed the need for independent inspection of public services 'to reassure the public and encourage the best performance' (quoted in Bone, 1993). Given this point of view, it is rather surprising that the Secretary for National Heritage appears to have rejected the suggestion for such a body made in the DNH public library review (Aslib 1995).

Such an organization would, however, have to be truly independent of government and not, as seems to be the case with OFSTED, simply be a mouthpiece for government policy, with the chief inspector providing, in the words of Professor Wragg, 'not an objective judgment but a political soundbite' (quoted in Hughill & Gold 1996). The government's main emphasis, for example, has been on value for money. There is a dangerous and persuasive simplicity about this concept, but if we consider the values of those making the judgment matters become rather more complicated. Politicians of the Left and Right, for instance, are unlikely to agree on how much value is obtained from expenditure on services that seek to prioritize the most needy in the community.

2   The professionals and others who work for and within the organization, and deliver the service. This may include anyone whose organizational role is to make decisions about the nature of the service delivered. The professionals' assessment of quality may be based on an approach which includes the development of service standards. These may, indeed, be produced by a national or international professional association. The government's charter initiative has seen the proliferation of customer charters and contracts in public libraries, which have often contained or referred to professionally established standards. As can be seen from Figure 4.3, 64% of respondents to the present study felt that the Citizen's Charter and library charters had been a significant force for change in the past five years.

The Library Association (1994a) in response to a ministerial challenge, has issued a *Charter for public libraries*. This was followed by a *Model statement of standards*, which is intended to help local authorities develop standards appropriate to their local circumstances (Library Association 1995). In addition, codes of good practice and policy documents containing local service standards have been produced by individual organizations.

Internally, service specifications may be produced. These have become common in the UK because government legislation requires public bodies to open up certain services to competition from the private sector through the process of compulsory competitive tendering (CCT). The London Borough of Brent voluntarily contracted out the running of two of its most successful branch libraries in 1994 and, as Chapter 8 indicates, we cannot be sure that CCT for library services is entirely off the Conservative Party's agenda. As suggested earlier, a

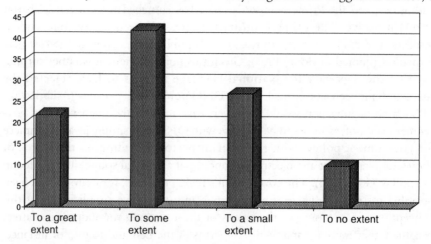

Fig. 4.3 Influence of citizen's library charters

detailed and comprehensive service specification defining the quality of the service to be delivered is an essential prerequisite of contracting out.

3 The users and 'customers' of the service. Although, as a subsequent chapter will indicate, the author dislikes the use of the word 'customer', most of the quality gurus stress the importance of taking what they call 'a customer-focused approach' to quality. This is because in private industry profits rely upon sales, which in turn rely upon retaining satisfied customers. As we have seen, the 'excellence' approach advocated by Peters and Waterman (1982) particularly emphasizes this aspect of a quality system.

However, even in the for-profit sector consultation with customers is not without its problems. The director of quality and strategy of a motor vehicle manufacturer recently told library researchers:

> Of course we consult widely; it is important to do so but we do recognize that there are limitations. The greatest problem is that human beings are usually limited by their own experiences and we find that their expectations of what they want in a new car are way too low, they only want something that is a little bit better than what they've got (quoted in Milner et al. in press).

Such a view is supported by recent research in the general business environment. Palmer (1996), for example, is of the opinion that:

> Marketing has moved on from being a set of techniques which drew in customers . . .

In the public service sector the situation is even more complex. Although it can be said that the primary purpose of any public body is to meet the needs of citizens, there is seldom a direct relationship between an expressed need or demand for a service and the organization's ability to satisfy it. This can lead to tensions if the users of a service have been involved in setting service standards: their expectations may be far too high for the organization to deliver. As Bone (1993) picturesquely puts it, 'You cannot specify the sausage unless you know what the sausage machine can make'. Unfortunately, high expectations are not common among library users: too often they appear to be happy with a cheap sausage, whereas some librarians have followed the route of Macdonaldization and sought to provide bibliographical burger bars (*cf.* Hoggart 1991).

Public library users' perceptions of quality may be at odds with the standards of the professionals. Taylor (1993), in his regular 'Quality Street' column in the *New Statesman*, makes the point that customers have been found to want a social relationship rather than a perfect service. Morgan and Potter (1995) argue that 'politicians, clients, purchasers/commissioners and provider organizations may have quite contradictory ideas about what constitutes quality within health care'. Similarly different perceptions have been revealed by the DNH public library review. In this the data show that most users thought the services had improved over the past few years, whereas most of the professionals questioned thought it had deteriorated.

Stewart and Walsh (1989) have also pointed out that it is not always clear who the customer is. In the case of a centrally maintained school library service, for instance, is the customer the child, the school, individual teachers or the local education authority that funds it? The perception of quality held by these diverse groups is likely to vary considerably. If the customer is a corporate user of the service, the position is much more straightforward. The answer here may be to negotiate the quality of service and establish a service level agreement in partnership with the client department or service.

A very helpful analysis of what dimensions of quality may be based on user perceptions and requirements is contained in Stewart and Walsh's (1989) pamphlet for the Local Government Training Board (LGTB). Stewart has written:

> Patients in a hospital may be able to judge how they feel after an operation but do not have the knowledge or ability to judge how effectively the surgeon has performed. Only the surgeon or a colleague may have that knowledge.

Similarly, a library user may be satisfied with the stock in her or his library but only a librarian may have the knowledge to judge the breadth, depth and accuracy of the range of material on offer. On the other hand, if we consider the experience of the user, for example, in terms of his or her across-the-counter encounters, then clearly he or she has the knowledge to be involved in an assessment of the quality of the interaction. Thus, rather than expecting every stakeholder in the public library to be able to judge the whole service, we need to distinguish between their ability to judge, the quality of the services offered, the quality of the environment in which the service is offered, the quality of the service relationships, and so on.

Some of the more thoughtful writers on quality have stressed the importance of asking such fundamental questions. Kano (1995), for example, quotes the Konica company, which asked 'Why does the customer buy a camera?' This led to a discussion of the situation in which consumers took pictures, and an investigation at process laboratories of the causes of picture failure. The problems identified led to the development of automatic focus, automatic film loading/winding etc. and a much more successful camera. Kano lists the key points of 'attractive quality' creation as:

- Concentrate on the purpose of using a product/service rather than the product/service itself.
- Listen to various voices about how the product is used
- Add our own creative thinking.

- Verify by a survey of many customers.

In the public library context we too should concentrate on and define the purpose of the service, listen to various voices and add our own professional creative thinking. In asking who judges the quality of the service, we should then consider:

- the extent to which the user can assess the service;
- the extent to which professional librarians can assess the service;
- the extent to which other stakeholders, such as local politicians, can assess the service.

The answers may of course vary with the different aspects of the service to be evaluated and the different attitudes of those approaching the task, including writers of professional texts.

As we have seen, the concept of quality has produced a considerable amount of literature which tends to be dominated by a small number of gurus. The danger is that librarians, in common with many others responding to the pressures of the Citizen's Charter initiative, will turn to these gurus and implement their ideas in a rather mechanistic way. In so doing they may fail to consider the relevance or otherwise of the various quality approaches to the needs and values of public service. The work carried out for the Sheffield/Loughborough project indicates that much further work is required before we can be said to have developed an approach that is properly suited to the needs of the public library.

Chapter 5

Communicating with the client

P UBLIC LIBRARIANS WERE interested in their users long before the Citizen's
Charter, quality councils and the award of Charter marks. True, Maurice
Line once suggested that the history of librarianship was a history of ignoring the user (Line 1980), but that was some time ago and in recent years the user
has hardly been ignored, at least if one looks at the professional literature. Public
library user surveys have been carried out since the 1950s and earlier. They
appeared in great profusion in the 1960s and 1970s and there has been a steady
stream ever since. Indeed, it is 20 years since the Centre for Research on User
Studies was established at Sheffield University. During the more recent past the
views of different communities of users have been obtained through studies that
have examined public opinion on public library services. As is noted in Appendix
I, users were a major focus of the DNH review (Aslib 1995).

Even if we admit that good practice has not always followed good theory, the
library profession can take some pride in its various attempts to reflect users'
interests and needs. In fact, one is tempted to argue that the public relations
rhetoric of today's entrepreneurial librarians does rather less for the user than the
solid professional reality provided by the library pioneers of an earlier age.

That having been said, all local government services are being urged to consult
more with their users. In the public library service, as elsewhere, such consulta-
tions have increased in number. Figure 5.1 shows that 86% of the respondents to
the present study felt that such activity had increased over the past five years.
Although such consultation has an important public relations function, we do
need to be aware of accepting the consumerist perspective in its entirety. In the
words of Roberts (1986), 'assigning consumers a watch-dog role is not necessarily a decision that leads to improved services or, even, to a fuller reflection of user
needs'. As indicated elsewhere in this text, the matter is complicated by the perhaps conflicting needs of the collective and individual user. Indeed, even in the
private sector:

> Traditional definitions of marketing based on the primacy of meeting cus-
> tomer's needs are increasingly being challenged by the requirements to satisfy
> the needs of wider stakeholders in society (Palmer 1996).

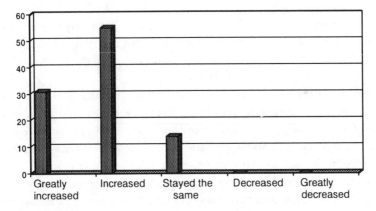

Fig. 5.1 *Consultation with users*

However, as is argued in the previous chapter, the individual client is well placed to judge the quality of his or her interactions with library staff. In common with many other organizations, libraries have recently invested significant resources in developing customer care and other programmes designed to improve the quality of these encounters. The idea of customer care is not a particularly new one for the library profession. Over 100 years ago a librarian by the name of Samuel Svett Green (1876) addressed a professional conference on 'The desirableness of establishing intercourse and relations between librarians and readers in popular libraries'. He was concerned, as should be today's professionals, with our relationships with people.

In the first place there are the internal relationships between the people who work in libraries, and secondly there are external relationships between librarians and their clients. As these sets of relationships are examined it should become clear that a successful external relationship with the people who use or could use library services depends on there being a successful internal relationship between the staff who work in them. There are some echoes here of the internal customer concept to be found in the literature of quality management. This was, however, predated by a professional writer (Fontaine 1975) who referred to the tick/click philosophy. She argued that without that internal tick generated by open communications and understanding within the organization itself, there can be no external click out there in the community.

However, if, to use Halmos' (1970) phrase, librarians are members of the personal service professions, they need to communicate with their clients at a rather deeper level than that implied by the concept of 'customer care'. In this section we concentrate on those matters that can help the public librarian get closer to the user of the service in the sense that she or he can develop an empathy with the user, for despite the reservations outlined earlier, the client is the most important person in any public library service. This is not to say that he or she is, in the simplistic marketing sense, always right, but that professional librarians must develop effective techniques to understand and serve their needs. These, as we have seen, might be different from their wants.

For the purposes of this discussion we shall assume that the service is presented in an appropriate and attractive way, and that the organization has an effective and efficient communications network and that members of staff are aware of policies, the management philosophy and the full range of services on offer, that is, that the generic aspects of good management have been taken care of.

If the library service is not meeting those criteria it is operating under a severe handicap, because good continuous communication is a way of avoiding the misunderstandings that can seriously damage an organization's internal and external relationships. The success or failure of such communication depends to a large extent on the attitudes of management: the ability to keep communication channels clear is one of the most important and potentially productive skills that a public library manager can possess.

A decade or more of customer care training has convinced most public librarians that their relationship with their clients is crucial. but a great deal of the training has been at a rather superficial level. Although there is nothing particularly wrong with 'Have a nice day' and the 'smiling negative' we need also to examine the relationship between staff attitudes and the effective – or otherwise – delivery of public library services.

Attitudes play an important part in interpersonal communication. None of us can take part in the work process without colouring it to some extent with our own attitudes. Members of staff do not leave their attitudes at the entrance with their coats, they bring them into the workplace. The relationship between attitudes and behaviour is a complex one that cannot be explored here, but it is true to say that attitudes can and do predispose people to perceive and behave in certain ways.

Our individual attitudes may be the result of self-interest, beliefs, reputation or the code of the society in which we live and work. Whatever their function, attitudes will affect the way clients are dealt with. Members of staff cannot always change their attitudes, but they do need to be aware of them and the prejudices they might conceal.

There are a number of techniques to help them do this. In classes at Sheffield the author sometimes asks students to make a list of 'the sort of people who annoy me', or ' the sort of people I don't like', and to consider how their personal prejudices might affect face-to-face encounters with members of the public. Some organizations, including public libraries, have formalized this kind of activity by asking their staff to complete 'values clarification' and/or 'attitudes to readers questionnaires'. Thus staff are asked to answer 'yes' or 'no' to questions such as, 'Do you think marijuana should be legalized?'; 'Are you willing to admit when you are wrong?'; and 'Do you think sex education in schools should include techniques for contraception?' Questions designed to clarify staff/reader relationships ask staff to answer 'yes, no or uncertain' to such statements as: 'Do you feel embarrassed if you are asked about a subject you have never heard of?'; or 'You are justified in losing your temper with a reader when he/she makes unreasonable demands.'

What is important in this kind of exercise is not so much the answers but the meaning of those answers in terms of staff relationships with clients. By increasing their awareness of themselves and their emotions, library staff will also increase their awareness of other people. People on counselling courses are sometimes asked to complete the segments of an 'awareness wheel' (Figure 5.2) to identify triggers that might make them angry, embarrassed, distressed or frightened.

It helps to be fully aware of our own feelings in any encounter. Each of us tends to see things in terms of our own dominant needs, views and prejudices, and this can lead to very real communications problems. Each one of us can identify certain subjects, ideas, groups or personalities that set off our emotional trip wires. In the work situation this can become personalized and individualized so that a particular member of staff or of the public can trigger such a reaction. The stronger these feelings are the less likely the chance of any kind of mutual understanding and communication. Everyday occurrences can have an emotional content, at least for some people, and attitudes, emotions and ideas of rational action are mixed up together in all of us.

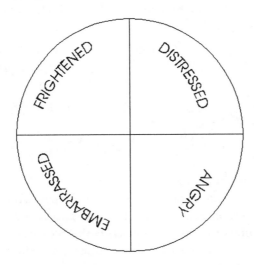

Fig. 5.2 *The awareness wheel*

There is a wide range of learning materials to help librarians understand this process and the impact it can have on an interaction. These include values clarification tests, self-analysis quizzes, attitude questionnaires, interpersonal relationship scales, awareness wheels, case studies, trigger videos and a variety of role-playing exercises.

In addition, the literature on the shelves of public libraries provides many opportunities to help increase our acceptance and understanding of a wide range of people and their emotions. Books, plays, films and poetry can all provide insights into people's lives and help us be more open with those people we seek to serve. The writer Barry Hines has written quite directly on the problems readers can have when using libraries. In *Unfinished business* he describes the problems of a working-class woman attempting to use a university library:

> Lucy had not known how to use the library at first. She was frightened of it. Three floors of books and a basement of old journals were too much for her. She had been put off libraries when she was a little girl . . . But she had been forced to use the university library when she needed a book. [She tries to find the book] There seemed to be no logic to the numbers on the shelves 500 10 20 30. She reached the end and turned the corner . . . 603 603? She looked around, where was 540? She never found it. It was like standing at a crossroads not knowing which road to take. She asked the library assistant . . . the girl pointed vaguely ahead. 'Along there . . . Next to architecture, I think'. Lucy never found architecture. She started to sweat. She felt like crying. She wanted to go home.

She eventually, although not without difficulty, finds the book and attempts to take it out:

> The librarian asked her for her ticket. She said she hadn't got one. She felt angry and embarrassed as if being wrongly accused of shoplifting. Was she a student? Yes. The librarian demanded proof. Lucy produced her union card and the librarian, . . . sent her across to another desk to register. After receiving her tickets, there was only the electronic security system and the porter's search to negotiate as she went out. At last she had done it. She had borrowed a book! She walked down the steps drained but elated. She knew how a bank robber must feel after making a successful getaway. (Hines 1983).

Such insights are not, unfortunately, provided by the popular press. Newspapers such as *The Sun* or *Daily Mail* simply exploit prejudices and present us with a very narrow view of the world. If any readers of this book take them, they should cancel them right away. Of course, such a statement may reflect the prejudices of the author. However, by coming to terms with our own prejudices, problems and difficulties we are in a much stronger position to establish a rapport and effective working relationship with the client.

Many clients do have very real problems in using public libraries. There are problems of physical and psychological access to information. For example, the simple (or apparently simple) action of asking a question can be seen as revealing one's ignorance. To reverse the coin for a moment: some members of staff may be afraid of revealing their own ignorance when faced with a question or enquiry that they fear is too difficult or technical. In addition, when the public library service becomes involved in an area such as community information, other problems can arise: the client may be revealing psychologically damaging details about his or her personal circumstances; others may be simply frightened by organizations that they might perceive to be too authoritarian, too posh, or whatever. Some people may have had bad experiences on previous visits to other agencies, and they may bring this negative expectation through the doors of the public library. For many clients these problems are increased by physical, educational, emotional or economic handicaps. Developments such as the so-called 'care in the community' also mean that we must take steps to welcome into our libraries people who behave strangely, and allow them their right to be different.

Thus the use of a public library can involve a considerable psychological and emotional investment on the part of clients. If they are then made to feel that their request is a waste of time, they may not ask for help again. If they are made to feel unwelcome or a nuisance they will probably not return.

Many years ago some public library staff went on strike because they were accused by a councillor of not smiling. Whatever the rights or wrongs of that particular case, the council member was correct to recognize the importance of smiling and other non-verbal communication. The whole topic has been well covered in general terms by Michael Argyle (1990), Desmond Morris (1994) and others, and in the context of libraries by a British Library report (Levy & Usherwood 1992). There is, then, no need to go into detail here, but suffice it to say that non-verbal communication plays a significant part in establishing social relationships. Words, too, can be used to establish rapport between people. One writer (Sapir 1971) has referred to the 'caressing or reassuring quality of speech'. This can be seen in the 'small talk' that manifests itself in many social situations, including those that take place across the desk or counter in a public library.

It is, then, quite proper that staff should be encouraged through training to meet and greet clients. A friendly smile and a word of greeting can only help a person feel more welcome and more at ease. This perhaps is especially true as the new technology begins to take over. This is a point recognized by banks, who have tried to humanize their automated systems by placing a great deal of emphasis on 'customer care'. They have realized that there will be times when clients just want to talk to another human being. A student at Sheffield summed up the limitations of IT during a discussion about the use of expert systems, when she said 'You know . . . a machine can't see somebody cry'. Technically they probably can, or soon will be able to, but readers will understand the real significance behind that statement.

Public library clients come from a range of socioeconomic, cultural, educational and other backgrounds. These too can affect an interaction. Some readers may remember the BBC television programme 'Crosstalk', which showed an ill-tempered encounter between a bank clerk and an Asian customer. The problem was shown to be caused by a cultural mismatch of non-verbal signals, in this instance the tone of voice. To the clerk the Asian sounded rude, but, as the programme demonstrated, this was not the case: the clerk had simply misinterpreted the intention of the client's intonation. The same thing can and does happen in public libraries. To help overcome such difficulties some organizations now include racial awareness in their training programmes.

It is also necessary to consider the level and the complexity of the language used in our communication with clients. This is important both in terms of face-to-face encounters and in any publications that we might produce. The real aim of the public librarian in getting close to the user should be to establish a good rapport and effective relationship. This is often easier said than done, but can be achieved by giving him or her your full attention, through active listening and by responding in a genuine and accepting way. Giving a person your full attention requires practice. Try it. Try it now. Try it tonight. Practise giving your complete attention to another person. Try and suspend your own concerns and tune in completely to the other person. Try and get behind their feelings and reflect back to them what they are saying and feeling. Active listening involves paying this kind of attention, paraphrasing the client's concerns and asking open questions that will move the encounter forward.

However, even when management pays close attention to interpersonal skills training and the other things discussed in this chapter, there will be some dissatisfied and difficult clients. Some techniques for dealing with this situation have been outlined elsewhere (Usherwood 1981), so suffice it to say that complaints received by an organization should be taken seriously and used constructively. They are, after all, a manifestation of one client's dissatisfaction with the service. Moreover, a complaint from just one client may be an indication of a more widespread lack of satisfaction. Much of the present text is critical of people in the public services who simply adopt commercial models of management, but in this case it may be possible to learn something from those hotels and airlines whose quality systems include soliciting comments and suggestions from users on the range and quality of services offered, and the helpfulness of the staff delivering them.

More difficult situations are the subject of the CAB video Face to Face. This is an excellent training aid, which has been used by the author with a variety of groups. In essence, it gives people the opportunity to think about how they would deal with a series of clients whose actions are presented on a television screen. Participants in the training sessions are asked to consider their own feelings, and to discuss what it is about the client that they are reacting to. For instance, are they reacting to the client's physical appearance, mood, actions or language? They are then asked to contemplate whether their personal feelings are so strong that they have to turn away, physically or mentally, from attempting to meet the client's needs. Trainees are then asked to say what they would do in the different situations shown in the video, that is, how they would respond to the client, and how, after consideration, they wish they had responded. They are also asked to evaluate their own feelings: are they hostile or unsympathetic to the client? If so, would they be able to put such feelings aside and help the client, and how might they put the client at ease? Last, but not least, they are asked to think about the client, to consider why she or he is acting in the way they do? What does the client expect the information worker to do, and what is he or she feeling? Words alone cannot do justice to this particular learning experience, but it is strongly recommended as a useful and involving training aid.

This chapter began with a reference to a paper presented over a century ago. A more recent piece by Harris (1988), dealing with a type of service very much of this century, reaffirms many of Green's conclusions, albeit in a very different context. In a fascinating study of the information needs of battered women, she concluded that:

> Regardless of the specific information or assistance sought, if it was delivered with sensitivity in a warm non-judgmental way, the women felt they had been helped by the contact. Therefore, if librarians are to be of assistance to battered women, it is essential that they not only be able to provide accurate and appropriate information, but that they can demonstrate basic listening skills in their interactions with these women.

Although such findings are obviously applicable to community information services, they also have relevance to a wider range of public library activities. Halmos (1970), to whom we have already referred, has written that:

> All personal service professionals are either already interested in social sciences or becoming interested in it . . . they are concerned to find out about the social background and history of their clients. They are also increasingly conscious of the fact that their own relationship with their clients is complex . . . Indeed, they recognize that rendering effective help to their clients, while

remaining only intuitively sensible of social realities, is no longer thought satisfactory . . . in the personal service professions.

This quotation comes from over a quarter of a century ago, and reflects a much more sophisticated approach to clients and users than is covered by some of the more glib exponents of customer care training. Some readers may find it difficult to translate Halmos' ideas to a time when sociology and compassionate assistance to the less advantaged, not to mention professionalism itself, are under attack. Such a perspective is essential if we are to rediscover our professional purpose. However, these days, as the next chapter shows, we are in danger of evaluating library services in a rather different way.

Part 3

Values or money?

Arithmetic has its uses, but neither the injuries inflicted by inequality nor the benefits conferred by diminishing it can be reliably explained by sums in long division.
In reality, the consequences of social expenditure depend, not merely on its amount, but on the character of the evils removed and the opportunities opened by it.   R. H. TAWNEY, *Equality*, 1975

Chapter 6

Managing and measuring performance

A S POLLITT (1988) has written, 'the literature on *how* to measure, and the methodology of performance measurement, vastly exceeds that on *why* or *for whom* we should measure'. Given the profession at which this book is aimed it is not necessary to repeat the material that colleagues can find for themselves. Over the years the literature of librarianship, if not the practice, has contained references to a wide range of evaluation methods. The older readers of this text will recall techniques that hid behind mysterious abbreviations such as MBO (Management by Objectives), PPBS (Planning, Programming, Budgeting Systems) and OR (Operational Research). More recently we have seen the development of techniques such as business process re-engineering, performance-based budgeting and investment decision making. This chapter, however, will place rather more emphasis on the why and for whom than the how.

Increasingly the profession is being asked to prove that services are providing value for money, and/or that they are being provided in the most cost-effective way. The setting of output or outcome standards or measures has become a way of life for the public library manager. Figure 6.1 shows that over 90% of respondents to the survey undertaken for this publication feel that this kind of activity has increased in the past five years.

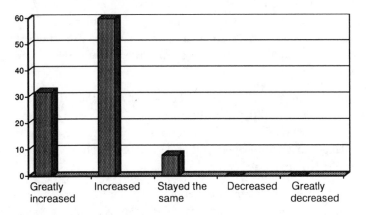

Fig. 6.1 *Setting of output measures*

In a recent response to the public library review and the KPMG report on contracting out, Virginia Bottomley (1995) said that, 'Like all public services, libraries must justify the level of financial support they receive and express clearly their role, in terms which can be easily understood'. In essence there is little to criticize in such a view: the public has a legitimate interest in the inputs (their taxes) to, and the outcomes of, public library services. In addition, most professionals want to evaluate services so as to prove their value, improve their performance, increase their effectiveness and plan for future developments.

There is general agreement that it is a management responsibility to evaluate public library services, or at least to have them evaluated. By evaluation we mean assessing their effectiveness. This assumes making a judgment against a standard, goal or yardstick. However, such evaluation must be much more than mere measurement. To advocate quantitative detachment beyond a certain point has little merit. Statistics are just a small part of the reality of the public library and any meaningful evaluation has to go beyond simplistic quantification.

Academic library colleagues, via the Follett Report (Joint Funding Councils 1993), have observed that 'relatively little attention has been paid to qualitative measures, or to output measures, but indicators which fail to take such factors into account will be inadequate and misleading'. In the public sector it has also been argued that 'performance can seldom be expressed in a meaningful way by quantitative data only. To a great extent, analysis of performance has to be based on qualitative descriptions and statements' (Arvidsson 1986).

The trouble is that in the present political climate library professionals have to make public libraries understandable to people who feel that nothing is of use unless it can be measured, preferably in terms of money. According to the New Right, the

> . . . basis of evaluation of anyone should be what other people are prepared to pay for their goods and services. In this sense moral merit or desert does not matter. What matters is the result of a person's endeavours and whether others are prepared to pay for it. This is the only criterion of value in a free society (Hoover & Plant 1989).

Such a statement illustrates the size of the gap between the values of the private and public sectors. It is difficult to justify what public libraries do to people with such a blinkered view of the world. In an organization where cost is everything there is a danger that commitment and pride will be forgotten. As the Director of Boston Public Library has written:

> An institution which is largely the embodiment of intangible values can only be diminished when a material monetary standard is applied to every function, when only that which is tangibly measured is valued (Curley 1989).

Public libraries generate benefits to the community at large. They benefit more than the individual user or taxpayer, and performance indicators should be designed to take account of this.

Even Deming, who is often associated with the use, if not the overuse of statistics, has admitted that the most important things in life cannot be measured. How does one measure love, kindness and generosity? Many of the measures that are set out in the managerialist literature are substitutes for qualities that are intangible or indirect. Moreover, the results of such an accountant's view of the world are often misleading in terms of assessing the real quality and impact of the service that is provided.

In criticizing this approach we are not saying that economy, or indeed the rest of the Audit Commission's three Es, is unimportant, but that they need to be considered in the context of the broader purpose of the public library. Even relatively crude indicators, such as numbers of staff, can provide valuable information if they are used in the right way. Research (Yates 1983) has shown how many of the recent tragedies in the national health service could have been avoided if staff input figures had been treated as warning signs. However, we should not be surprised if accountants interpret data in a different way from professionals. For the accountant empty hospital beds are seen as 'spare capacity'; for the doctor they are a safety net that has to be there in case of an emergency.

Recently, in Britain we have seen how the privatized utilities have failed to cope with the British climate because they had reduced their staff numbers. An interpretation of staffing figures that looked to the needs of users rather than shareholders might have helped prevent this. Efficiency is a significant factor in the management of an organization, but it has to be considered alongside the specific needs to be satisfied. Thus for the gas and electric companies the primary consideration should have been to maintain the service to the public, rather than cut costs so as to improve dividends for shareholders. Similarly, in the case of the public library the choice of measures used, and the way that they are used, needs to be in line with the policies and values that govern the public library service.

In the past public libraries, like many other public services, have been judged on the level of the resources they received and the magnitude of their acquisitions. The continuous financial cutbacks imposed by central government have caused local councils to require, and indeed provide, greater accountability for how money is spent. Local councillors and the professionals they employ now have to justify the allocation of resources by demonstrating the value of their outcomes.

However, the value of public library services cannot be established in the same way as their cost. It is not hard to ascertain the number of staff or the size of the stock, but rather more difficult to measure user satisfaction or the quality of the service. As Giappiconi (1995) argues:

Gathering favourable opinions from indicators such as 'degree of user satisfaction' in general or even 'degree of user requirement satisfaction' does not in itself have much significance. For example, are contented users satisfied with the charm of the librarian or with the effectiveness of the services?

Generally rather more is known about input than output and outcomes. Library managers know the cost of a book, a journal subscription or an online search, but cannot be sure in advance of their value to present or future users. If public library services are to be evaluated in terms of their impact on individuals and society as a whole then we are going to require sociological and psychological research skills. It means that we must be concerned with the 'soft' as well as the 'hard' areas. As Stewart and Ranson (1988) have observed:

> Performance monitoring in the public domain is not merely concerned with effectiveness in achieving stated values, but with unexpected impact, and of values denied.

It is a great pity that so much library evaluation underemphasizes value. Because figures are relatively easily available, the majority of exercises to determine the effectiveness of library services have been concerned with counting the numbers of people using the service. Such head counting tells us relatively little about the value of the service. As Giappiconi (1995) reminds us:

> A loan is a loan, unquestionably. But the loan of *Tristam Shandy* . . . or of a quality children's book does not have the same significance as the loan of a Barbara Cartland.

Equally, it may take the same effort on the part of professionals to issue ten books in one kind of neighbourhood as just one in another. It was this that led the author, when in practice, to suggest (not entirely with tongue in cheek) that the libraries with the lowest issues should employ the greatest number of professional staff.

'In a management culture where only numbers count, the uncountable is not only illegitimate it is insignificant as well' (Tusa, quoted in Porter 1995). When the number of people passing through the system becomes an end in itself, then such evaluation can be very dangerous indeed. Gaster's (1995) research in the health service illustrates this point. She recalls a time when:

> I naively asked what were FCEs and why they were important. It turned out . . . that they were 'finished consultant episodes' (death or discharge in former terminology) and were the basis of payments to potential providers of health care. Turnover, not results, was the thing.

In our own field, although a great amount of work has been carried out on 'the user', we still know relatively little about the functions of library materials in terms of their impact on the user. A model for the kind of work that could be undertaken can be seen in the 'uses and gratification studies' carried out by those involved in mass media research. The recent public library review did something to discover what public library users themselves consider important about books, periodicals, compact discs and so forth, but much more research remains to be done. Such information has obvious practical implications for libraries in, for example, the creation of stock development and selection policies. Similarly, in evaluating and planning services for communities there are techniques such as cognitive mapping which may help library managers gain a clearer impression of people's perceptions of an area or locality.

As the Comedia report (*Borrowed time* 1993) stated:

> The role of the library in community development and enrichment is a vital issue, but one which is not easily amenable to current concerns with 'performance indicators'. Such techniques can easily measure book issues, turnover of book stock and other statistics, but in no way can measure the quality of the relationship between a library, its users and the geographical area it serves.

This was an argument that was revisited in their more recent work, *Libraries in a world of cultural change*. This showed that much more empirical work is needed, and suggested that the library community initiate research on the economic and social impact of the public library (Greenhalgh et al. 1995). One respondent to the present study agreed saying:

> I believe that much of the effort towards specifying and quantifying services is searching for something entirely illusory, i.e. there may be better, more subjective ways of determining quality. We have been over obsessed with specification etc. (Welsh county)

Public libraries, according to one respondent, are 'distinctively different in tenor of service value and ethos. We are still not dividend led. Therefore we must work harder at our own relevant performance measuring' (English county). Another argued that 'Public libraries generally need to focus on performance measurement which is meaningful to the user (i.e. qualitative) rather than convenient in Audit Commission terms' (English county). The present author has for a number of years suggested that this kind of research be carried out via a 'social process audit' (Usherwood 1989). This is a

> . . . dynamic technique that goes far beyond a kind of bottom line approach to evaluation and managerial control. It seeks to provide managers with a technique that will enable them to determine whether [a] program is being implemented effectively, how it can be improved, and generally whether the

program is worthy of continuation according to their particular standards (Blake et al. 1976).

At the time of writing the British Library has awarded a grant to Sheffield University to carry out a social audit of libraries in Newcastle and Somerset.

The technique has much in common with quality audits as defined by Percy-Smith and Sanderson (1992) and implemented by a number of local authorities with regard to recreation, transport and information technology services. The social audit is a practical strategic management tool, allowing an assessment of social costs and benefits and encouraging greater social gains. It is currently being used by a variety of voluntary organizations and companies such as Traidcraft and the Body Shop. To quote Gray (1995), social accounting has experienced 'a (long overdue) resurgence as academics . . . look for new ways of providing accounts of organizational life'. The technique can be used to examine the success or failure of a portfolio of activities and services offered by a particular kind of library, for example inner city, urban or rural branch libraries, or those serving designated areas of poverty.

Most modern statements of public library purpose imply that it is the function of the public library to provide equality of access to information. For example, the UNESCO Public Library Manifesto published in 1994 states that, 'The services of the public library should be provided on the basis of equality of access for all regardless of age, race, gender, religion, nationality, language or social status'. The success or otherwise of such a policy could be evaluated by an investigation of the economic and social impact of library policies on different sections of the community; this could help ascertain the degree to which taxes paid by different social groups relate to the benefits these groups receive from library and information services. It is, of course, recognized that not every user is a taxpayer. In addition to providing information about the direction and equity of the 'tax burden', such an investigation could provide data on the differences in physical, psychological and economic access to libraries. The audit could also provide further information about the extent to which libraries are, in the current climate, attempting or withdrawing the provision of facilities for those who are not, or unlikely to be, users of public library services.

Such an analysis could then reveal the balance in the distribution of public library services. It may well raise fundamental questions regarding the equity of the present provision of services and the methods used to fund them. In some places significant questions are being asked about the relevance of inner city services. For example, in some authorities inner city libraries have higher staffing ratios but little is known as to what value, if any, these posts add to the service. More generally, information is needed on the impact of library services on other council services and policies. In Newcastle, for instance, the city has a range of strategies to combat disadvantage. These range from economic regeneration to educational achievement, women's issues, community care, racial equality and disability. It is the aim of the library and information services in that city to affect all these policies.

Given these objectives, as defined by the City Council, the Sheffield University project will be used to evaluate the impact of library policy and services on the city centre and neighbouring communities. A comparative study in Somerset will provide an additional rural dimension to the project. In such areas there are different issues with regard to access (and equality of access) and impact. Social audit techniques can also be used to test a wide range of library policies and professional assumptions, for example the socioeconomic influence of specialized services to ethnic minorities and housebound people, the special nature of reading, and the role of libraries in promoting cultural appreciation.

Whereas populist slogans such as 'value for money' may attract some public support, a proper evaluation of the public library service demands a more thorough investigation and diagnosis of its contribution to society. As early as 1957 the leading management guru of the time, Simon, recognized that:

> Some substitute must be found in public administration for money value of outputs as a measure of value. This substitute is provided by a statement of objectives of the activity, and by the construction of indices that measure the degree of attainment of these objectives.

This message was repeated recently by Walsh (1995), who stated:

> The public sector, despite much searching, has signally failed to find an acceptable set of performance indicators. It may be that the search is futile because whether or not a policy is successful, at least in the short term, will itself be a matter of political construction.

Moreover, in looking at value for money the emphasis has tended to be more on monetary cost than community values. Ten years ago the National Consumer Council observed that:

> Value for money has degenerated into a catch phrase, used largely as a euphemism for providing services at the lowest possible cost, with scant regard for what services actually achieve. Of the three 'Es' attention is generally paid only to economy and efficiency. Service effectiveness is virtually ignored (quoted in Murray & Letch 1987).

The new managerialists have little time for ideas of equality or equal opportunity.

In 1992, under the auspices of the Citizen's Charter, the Local Government Act gave the Audit Commission the responsibility of drawing up a set of indicators to measure and compare the performance of local councils. These found favour with a minority of respondents to the present study, one observing: 'performance measurements introduced by bodies such as the Audit Commission are effective and could with profit be added to' (English metropolitan district). However, most feel that such comparisons are not well suited to much that we do. The extreme of this position is reflected in the comment that 'performance measurement is not a topic which interests me' (London borough).

Be that as it may, the Citizen's Charter has increased the emphasis on performance measurement and the growth of systems to help measure such performance. Such developments are not wholly bad in so far as they have caused the profession to consider and perhaps reconsider the real goals, outputs and outcomes of the public library service. They raise fundamental questions about the service: what, for instance, are the desired results of providing a library service? How do we know when these results have been achieved, and what does accountability really mean?

It is reasonable that such questions should be asked. The public library service is provided out of public funds and it is only right that attempts be made to demonstrate what citizens are getting from the use of such funds, how the service benefits the lives of individuals and groups in the community, and how efficiently and effectively funds are used. Serious difficulties arise, however, when managers try to answer these questions using inappropriate tools. For a number of respondents to the present study the Citizen's Charter performance indicators are just that. They are:

> . . . regarded as narrow, ineffective and designed to aid local authority 'bashing' through the production of league tables etc. rather than constructive ways of aiding performance management. (English metropolitan district)

There is a very real danger that librarians will count that which can be counted but ignore that which is important. The final outcomes resulting from the provision of public library services are frequently very difficult to ascertain and/or difficult to separate from other factors in society. For instance, some very sophisticated measures, well beyond the ken of number crunchers, will be required to demonstrate that Janet and John have become better or worse readers as the result of using, or not using, a public library.

There is a danger that the business plan has become a poor substitute for taking cultural and social decisions. To quote McKevitt and Lawton (1994), 'the concern with measuring performance and ensuring accountability through quantification represents a triumph of techniques over judgment', a statement that is given point by Alan Taylor's (1993) wry observation on stock selection:

> . . . the new teams went into interminable huddles to decide whether to buy one copy or two of the latest Iris Murdoch. They knew nothing about books

or their contents but they had algebraic formulae to prove that Barbara Taylor Bradford was more cost-effective than Saul Bellow.

This is an example of what one of the respondents to this study described as:

> The counter productive effect of lifting industrial models in management and measurement of performance and trying, in some cases ludicrously, to make these fit library provision and services, leading to contortions and distractions to achieve some sort of statistical and definable fit. (Scottish district)

However, for those of the new managerialist persuasion comparative statistics are a public sector substitute for competition:

> The current required performance indicators merely give a quantitative approach, showing raw data which can be, and has been, immediately put into league tables, which are of no significance and give no idea of the quality of services provided. (Scottish district)

The accountant mentality will ask, 'If an operation in Library A costs £x what does it cost in Library B?' The professional will of course recognize that it is possible to identify a number of factors that not only can, but should, make a difference to any comparative judgment. For example, an authority may incur extra costs providing a service to a multicultural community or a rural population. It is also quite legitimate for different local authorities to have different priorities in terms of the services they offer. What merit is there in comparing Sheffield with (say) Solihull if the different populations have elected councils with different political, economic and social priorities? In a public library social values should predominate over financial values, and this complicates the measurement process.

The public library service is above all about providing equality of access to information, ideas and works of imagination, and it is important that this is reflected in the way services are evaluated. This means that checks are required on physical access in terms of the buildings and vehicles that house library services. It will also mean 'measuring' the amount of access to materials in the various languages of the people who make up the community the library serves. In such circumstances it is important to know the racial, gender and age take-up of the public library service. User satisfaction surveys should be designed to take account of the experiences of different groups within the community. Data from such studies will help managers assess how far their services have penetrated different sections of the community. In looking for indicators of the equality of provision, a manager will need to consider the provision of equality-specific services, such as those aimed at meeting the the needs of sexual or racial minorities. He or she may also wish to find out whether, for example, working-class people find the library less relevant, or more difficult to use, than middle-class people.

Performance measures are not without a cost. It is estimated that the introduction of performance indicators cost the nation £20m in the first year (Jones 1995). Many may feel this is a high price to pay at a time when the public library service is so seriously underfunded. There is, said one respondent, a 'concentration on paper justification by outputs and performance measures at the expense of delivering the service' (English metropolitan district). As Jackson and Palmer (1992) indicate, 'care has to be exercised that all the costs of collection of all these permutations do not outweigh the usefulness . . . Performance measures do not in themselves provide solutions . . . They alert managers to the need to examine issues further.'

There may also be hidden costs in the way things get done as a result of an emphasis on measurement. This is particularly true if the act of measurement is perceived to be more important than the purpose of the service to be measured. A former senior finance director in the health service has admitted that, in order to meet the NHS target of treating people within a year, she had:

> . . . sat in rooms with purchasers saying that we have to give priority to somebody who has been waiting 12 months and that they don't care if somebody else, who may have been waiting three months, has to wait longer even though the clinicians say that could cause a disability' (Drown, quoted in Brindle 1996).

In addition, one wonders what have been the costs, in terms of the quality of the patient–doctor interaction, of measuring patient throughput?

There are other examples to be found in the public sector. What has been the cost to BBC programmes, in terms of their quality, of the growing emphsasis on audience size? In our own field, what has been the cost, in terms of the quality of library stock, of the stress on issue figures to justify purchase?

This overemphasis on measurement can lead to 'a fantasy world in which the statistics bear no relation whatever to what you are doing'. Moreover, the management effort that is spent on evaluation can be at the expense of other things. For instance:

> Britain's once admired academic standards . . . are fast declining (Elcock 1994) as ever increasing managerial 'exercises' and efforts to assess teaching and research distract academics from their proper role as seekers after and disseminators of knowledge (Farnham & Horton 1996).

As Stewart and Walsh (1994) have argued, excessively detailed performance measures can limit adaptiveness. In short, professionals can spend so much time justifying what they are doing that they do not have enough time to do it properly. This is certainly the experience of those currently working in universities, the health service and local government.

It is commonly said that what gets measured gets done. This is often true, but equally what gets done is not always central to the purpose of the organization. Potter (1988), referring to some earlier research with the health service, quotes a health manager who talked about evaluating the NHS on the quality of the custard rather than on its prime function to improve people's health. It is a moot point whether this is a cause or an effect of some hospitals concentrating on hotel rather than medical initiatives. In the health service as elsewhere, the Right has realized that 'managing appearances will be a fruitful strategy if it is only appearances that get measured' (Parker & Jary 1995). One of the respondents to the present study made a similar point, commenting on:

> . . . the greater emphasis on superficial output measures. An increase in PR level services which emphasize(s) superficial elements of the service (London borough).

In earlier research into standards (Stroud & Usherwood 1995) a respondent observed:

> I had to find money to buy plants and guiding. The staff were quite cynical about the whole thing, they viewed it as window dressing . . . staff would rather see the money spent on books (London borough).

The managing of public libraries' appearance via customer care courses, plants and similar window dressing initiatives may be one reason why so many members of the public responding to the public library review appeared to believe that the public library service has improved and is likely to do so in the next five years.

The reasons for this difference of perception are the subject of a further investigation (Wiles, 1996) but readers will immediately recognize the dangers of making management, or indeed political, decisions on the basis of such users' perceptions alone. Simply asking users about this kind of issue is often not enough. Users know what they like: they sometimes know what they need, but they often do not know what is possible for the library to provide. White (1985) has argued this point with some force, saying that when we ask users what they want they tell us what we have prepared them to tell us on the basis of low expectations.

A former Sheffield student (Worsfold 1994) provided an interesting perspective on why the users interviewed in the DNH survey thought public libraries had and would improve. They would, she said, have personal experience of using libraries and therefore have some relevant knowledge. However, their experience is characterized by being a snapshot: they do not spend all day and every day in the library, and they only see what is presented publicly to them by the library staff. They do not, for instance, see backroom backlogs. She went on to say that given the current drive for quality management, what the customers perceive has become a key issue. She recalled her own practical experience. In her library, she explained:

> Times were hard, but every single member of staff was sent on a two-day customer care course, and some of us were sent on a guiding course to improve layout and signing for all the libraries. Meanwhile the core service was in decline, with cuts in book-funds (which were not publicized), cuts in interlibrary loan services (which were not publicized), and cuts in opening hours. Perhaps the image that the customers were seeing was deceptive, the libraries *looked* better and the staff were well trained; however, customers do not count the number of new books on the shelves . . . perhaps quality management distorts the facts that users have available, causing positive impressions in spite of the decline.

This view was also put to the author by a senior practitioner at one of the many consultation meetings held on the DNH preliminary report.

Further explanation of the different perceptions between librarians and users may be found in the literature on the psychology of prediction. For instance, Slovic et al. (1982) and Tversky and Kahneman (1982) suggest that people judge events as likely if instances of them are easy to imagine or recall. What people can recall will depend on their knowledge and experience of the area. Library users, by definition, will have personal experience of using libraries. They will therefore have some relevant knowledge. However, as Stewart and Walsh (1989) suggest, from a different academic perspective, in a number of areas this knowledge will be incomplete.

As we have seen, Giappiconi (1995) has identified a number of similar problems caused by public librarians' overreliance on the customer-led entrepreneurial approach to evaluation. He warns against the dangers of the numbers game and argues that 'it is not the number of users which gives an institution its democratic character, but the fact that it serves the interests of the community (in particular the liberty and equality of the citizen)'.

Increasing the number of individual library users could be achieved relatively easily by appealing to the lowest common denominator, but offering the public library equivalent of *The Sun* or Sky television could not be called a public service in any sense of the word. Public libraries should be judged not simply in terms of efficiency and effectiveness, but by the degree to which they are contributing to their primary purpose, that is, why the library exists and what is its impact on individuals and groups in society.

To do this it is necessary to identify the desired outcomes of the library service before selecting the measures or indicators to be used. Professional bodies and individual authorities will need to set standards, not just for performance but also for outcomes. In identifying desired outcomes it is necessary to involve politicians, professionals, frontline staff and the users of the service. The measures and indicators selected must be appropriate for the service and community concerned. One must expect variations from authority to authority, but some indicators will be based on information about inputs to the service such as the amount spent on staff or books; information on outputs, such as the number of reference enquiries or books issued to a particular group; and information on outcomes. The latter might include such things as reading skills in the community, or quality outcomes such as the time taken to respond to complaints. The assessment of outcomes would particularly benefit from the use of the social audit techniques suggested above. Information on cost-effectiveness and efficiency will also be required. Crucially, all this information must be considered in the light of other information that will help to explain a library's performance. This could include such controllable factors as the age of library buildings or uncontrollable factors such as the size of minority ethnic communities.

The outcomes of the library service could then be compared with the standards set by the local authority and/or a professional association. It is now strongly argued that the results of this kind of exercise should be made publicly available and used in the future planning, management and improvement of the service. However, although it may also be useful to compare a library's performance with the 'best' libraries, the dangers of such simplistic comparisons need always to be borne in mind.

Benchmarking techniques may have something to offer here but as a forthcoming British Library report suggests:

> The process is a difficult one, and the benefits may not be apparent for some time, if at all. Where benchmarking is felt to be most useful, especially in the LIS sector, is as a means of raising staff awareness . . . The commercial emphasis on benchmarking against competitors, or world leaders, or the 'best of the best' may not provide a suitable framework for the LIS sector, as the culture is not, as yet, comparable with the with-profit sector (Garrod & Evans, in press).

There is now also a trend to measure the performance of individual members of staff and to reward them accordingly. In the survey carried out for this book, 39% of those responding held negative attitudes to individual performance related payments.

The data shown in Figure 6.2 reflect views to be found elsewhere in the library and information professions. In the special sector it 'is unpopular . . . it has done more to demoralize staff than to motivate them. Its effects can be particularly pernicious in small units dependent on team working and good interpersonal relationships' (Burge 1995). These comments are in line with research carried out elsewhere which suggests that performance-related pay works against

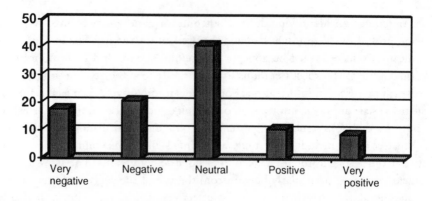

Fig. 6.2 *Attitudes to performance-related pay*

team working and discriminates against women. It is also in a significant way an insult to those who work in public service, and shows a lack of understanding of their motivation. As Flynn (1993) observes:

> To introduce performance related pay as though people's motivation to perform well was only determined by money will produce a demotivated workforce if they have other ideas.

It is the 'other ideas', such as fairness, equity and democracy that are, it would appear, beyond the ken of the managerialists of the New Right, who feel that workers have to be threatened or bribed.

In evaluating the performance of library services, and indeed the staff who work in them, there is a need to develop measures which provide some degree of understanding between the various stakeholders in the service. There will need to be provision for some communication and cooperation between these different groups. Measurement by itself will never improve the public library service. What is required is a strategy that uses the results of measurement to assess levels of service, and the improvements that are required for the future, improvements that may require more, rather than fewer, resources.

Chapter 7

Public choice or public voice?

THE TOTAL NET expenditure of the public library service in England and Wales in 1994/5 was £774.5m (CIPFA 1996). The service is provided for everyone at a net cost of less than 24 pence per person per week, or £12.24 per year. This cost has in fact fallen since 1991 when Comedia (*Borrowed time?* 1993) noted that it was £12.94 per head. At local authority level the public library service rarely accounts for more than 2% of a council's expenditure.

It is a service that, as the DNH public library review and other research shows, provides remarkable value for money and is valued by all sections of society. The New Right (Adam Smith Institute 1986) and public choice theorists find it convenient to portray the 'average user' of the public library as a wealthy person, but this is not the case, and there is a significant amount of work to prove otherwise. For instance, the MORI poll, carried out in 1992, showed that whereas 41% of users came from the A/B income groups, 20% of the most frequent users came from the poorest categories D and E. Similarly, work carried out by the Book Marketing Research Board (BMRB) found that 27% of frequent users came from the D and E groups and 81% from the C1, C2, and D/E groups (Van Riel 1992). These findings have been supported by more local research. Anstice (1994) found that in Newport, for example, 66% of users were earning less than £18,000 a year, with over a third earning less than £12,000. Thus in the words of the social historian Samuel (1992):

> Public libraries, unlike other major cultural institutions . . . have been from the start user friendly, accommodating a promiscuous mix of activity in their premises and ministering to what, in any given period, has been an astonishingly heterogeneous public.

If it is correct that a 'society affords what a society thinks is important' (Cram, in Booker 1993), then there is no doubt that the public supports the public funding of public libraries. The data obtained from surveys of users and non-users carried out for the DNH show:

- public support for public libraries;
- a favourable image of public libraries;

- public support for public funding;
- that the public feel that public libraries should be run by local authorities;
- little support for private companies running library services;
- support for new public library services.

Comments received by the Aslib team from members of the public, professionals and politicians, stressed that an educated electorate is essential for the full functioning of a democratic society. There is therefore support for strong central funding through general taxation – both to finance the infrastructure and to make services available to those unable to gain access via other means. Such sentiments were repeated time and time again in the evidence supplied to the review team.

For instance, a county librarian told the DNH consultants:

> It is important to recognize that it is only public funding which is likely to ensure service delivery in the spirit of freedom of information and equality of opportunity.

An individual user advised that:

> Economists might ponder the cost to the nation of an illiterate workforce, and accept that funding for libraries is a wise and necessary investment.

Given the current level of public library activities and the future potential of the service, it is clearly an underfunded national resource. This conclusion is supported by the DNH report and other research. Many respondents to the DNH review, and the survey carried out for this book, mentioned the crumbling infrastructure of public libraries. This they saw as the result of the economic neglect of recent years. Moreover there is evidence from the DNH data to suggest that the public would respond favourably to a modest increase in funding for the library service. Although at the margin there may be possibilities to raise extra funds through new partnerships, income generation, the national lottery and other diversified sources, the evidence clearly shows that the public library requires an injection of new public money.

The DNH review included a question on possible sources of funding for library services under pressure. This read: 'Suppose your public library needs extra resources to keep up services, to which one course of action would you give top priority?' Respondents were given a number of options, including raising the council tax, cutting back services and charging library users for all services, including book borrowing. This question was put to users and non-users of public libraries across the country and to professional librarians and other library staff in 12 case study areas. As the final report shows, there was clear support in all sectors for public funding. This support was most evident among professional librarians, and unsurprisingly, weakest among non-users of the service.

The DNH team also received many comments and submissions on the possibility of introducing direct charges for library services, and it is evident from these that librarians, library authorities and members of the general public across the nation are against any erosion of the free and open access that is characteristic of the British public library service. The following are typical of the many submissions received from groups and individuals:

I am somewhat concerned to learn that the public library service may in the future be funded by sources other than by public funds. (Member of the public)

The committee was against any charges for the loan of books. Any charge no matter how nominal would deter people from using libraries, especially children and people on low incomes. (****** Committee)

I am old enough to remember the recession in the 1920s and 30s; a very grim period. There was never any question of closing or having to pay for libraries. (Member of the public)

We also welcome the recommendation that the existing free core service provided by public libraries should be maintained, and in particular that a workable proposal is put forward for the extension of this principle to electronic information sources. (Library authority)

The principle of free and equal access to information, works of imagination and ideas is embodied in most contemporary statements of public library purpose. The 1994 UNESCO Public Library Manifesto quoted earlier provides a prime example of this. Such a principle is also in line with the present-day emphasis on citizenship. The National Consumer Council, in a much quoted report, stated that 'the other rights of citizenship are worth little without the right to education and information' (National Consumer Council 1977). The introduction of direct charges for public library services would, in practical terms, withdraw that right to information from many citizens.

This was recognized by many of those who gave evidence to the public library review, as the following submissions indicate:

I would hate to think that there was a direct charge as the gap between the 'haves' and the 'have nots' is already a huge one. In my youth and early days, the library was the *only* place I could read books, so I feel this should still be so, for the less financially secure folk. (Member of the public)

I feel that the government should leave local libraries local and make sure they do not squeeze finances too much that will cause councils to cut back on the service. (Member of the public)

I also abhor the idea of charges being made for [the] use of library facilities. There are too many families – adults, teenagers and children – suffering from cultural deprivation and to charge for the loan of books and other library uses would impoverish the nation still further. Better to seek more funding from e.g. the National Lottery – or could there not be a special 'Giving extra to the community' tax over and beyond the normal income tax, for people with income above a certain level, e.g. above £100,000 per annum? (Member of the public)

The library service is not free as we already pay for it through local taxation and I do not think users should be charged. There is a great and valid tradition that this source of information and learning is available for everyone regardless of means and it should remain so. It should not become an elitist service only for those who can afford it. (Member of the public.)

A recent article in the *Economist* made a similar point with regard to electronic sources of information:

There are several ways of trying to prevent the electronic age from widening the gap between the haves and the have-nots'. Public libraries offer one of the better ones . . . if access is not to be rationed by price, then another bottleneck is required: the need to go somewhere. People who want information badly enough to go out of their way for it should be able to get more free material than those willing only to click a switch at home.

Over the years the idea of public funding has ensured that 'any man or woman should be able to have any book for the asking – that his or her means of obtaining . . . reading should be as independent of the individual pocket as the lighting of the streets and drainage of the districts' (Greenwood 1891). For Greenwood that was 'the central idea' of the public library. Now, as then, it is clear that equality of access is important because information, reading and literacy skills are fundamental to people's life chances.

In the words of the Lacy Report (American Library Association 1986), 'How freely and equally citizens have access to knowledge determines how freely and how equally they can share in the governing of our society and in the work and rewards of our economy'. This message was repeated in the Comedia report, which observed that 'The library is based on the principle of borrowing from a common resource that is greater than any one individual or family could afford or accommodate' (*Borrowed time?* 1993).

This principle has been challenged to some extent in this country (Adam Smith Institute 1986) and to a greater degree in the United States (Weaver & Weaver 1979; White 1983). These writers have based their criticism of the free public library service on public choice theory. The world of public choice is, according to Walsh (1995), 'essentially a rational world, with everybody pursuing their own interests in the most efficient way, even when the result is social inefficiency'. Gosling (1993) has shown that 'the connecting philosophy behind the proposals of the ASI [Adam Smith Institute] is the theory of public choice: to take power away from officials and give it instead to the individual as consumer'. However, at best, consumer power rests on some shaky foundations. In the world of public choice a person is unlikely to be empowered unless they have money. The world of public choice is one in which the size of an individual's bank balance, rather than the collective voice of the ballot box, provides the passport to citizenship. As a result the poor – especially perhaps the information poor, as choice needs to be informed – lose their franchise. For most of us the past few years' apparent increase in our power as consumers has seen us lose democratic control of the things that affect us most. Choice is far from being the panacea that some of the Rightist theorists maintain.

A North American writer, Halliday (1992), has argued that 'economic theory can provide a rational perspective which offers some hope of reconciling these viewpoints'. However, Galbraith, one American economist who has specifically addressed the question of libraries, has long rejected the public choice approach. In 1979 he attacked those who maintained that the collective public library is against liberty. More recently he observed:

> There are some things the market system does not do either well or badly. In the good society these are the responsibility of the state . . . It must always be in mind that many of these parks and recreational facilities . . . libraries, the arts, are more needed by the underclass than the affluent (Galbraith 1994).

Galbraith's view is relatively rare among American economists, but that only serves to illustrate the political and cultural divide between this country and the United States. Many economic and social theories do not travel well across the Atlantic, a fact that is too often forgotten by Britain's New Right, who seem beguiled by Newt Gingrich et al. The differences between the culture in this country and that in the United States leads to differing responses to financial pressures. James Swan (1990), for example, believes that librarians across the United States can take advantage of a great potential for fundraising in libraries. He goes on to suggest that librarians and others interested in public libraries should go out and ask for support. Evidence supplied to the Aslib team suggested that, in America, advocacy by users and non-users resulted in a doubling of the per capita support for public libraries. Referenda for building or renovating public libraries between 1 July 1990 and 30 June 1991 had an 85% approval rate, which represented an improvement over recent years.

In this country, as we have seen, there is a greater expectation of public funding to support public services than is the case in America. Although it could be argued that for a brief period in the 1980s an obsession with money made some Britons more American in outlook, the recent British Social Attitudes (1994) shows that 'any perceived move against the welfare state as a whole . . . runs the risk of incurring the wrath of the electorate'. More recent research (*The glue that binds* 1996) has shown that:

> Ninety four percent of the British people believe that public services are essential in our modern society [and concludes] the prevalent views often run counter to the political and ideological arguments that have been used to advance and then defend so much public service reform over the past decade.

In cultural and professional terms British public libraries have more in common with those in Scandinavia. There, as Nilsson (1994) writes:

> The free of charge principle is central to most Nordic library legislation. It is upheld most strongly in Norway and Finland, although it has been somewhat relaxed in Finland in their last revision of 1992. Denmark amended its Library Act in 1993 and charges are made on recorded music, cassettes and videograms [sic].

Whereas this chapter has so far concentrated largely on matters of principle, a review of the literature indicates that considerable administrative difficulties would result from the introduction of charges. The effect on the national interlending system, the costs of collection, the effect on demand and so on have all been the subject of significant research. Most of the evidence, from the administrative perspective, also suggests that direct charges are not the answer to the funding problems facing the public library service. Some years ago the economics of charging were closely examined by the Association of County Councils (1980). This body concluded that 'the most efficient and economic way of paying for the [library] service is by way of rates and taxes rather than through any form of separate charge'. In a later report the Association of London Authorities Arts and Recreation Committee (1987) recommended 'that the principle of free access to library and information services be adopted as a fundamental policy'. Indeed, they went so far as to suggest the possible abolition of overdue, reservation, online and other charges. From a different political perspective, a Standing Committee of the Bow Group has 'concluded that the library service as presently constituted is the most effective way of providing books and information to the community (and that there would not be any widespread public or political support for the introduction of library charges)' (quoted in McKee 1987).

There is also a considerable body of evidence from outside Britain regarding the impact of charging on the use of public library services. In Nordrhein-Westfalen in Germany membership fell by 20% (75% in one library) when charges were introduced. There was a particularly sharp decline in use by poorer people. Leverkeusen suffered a similar fate, with a 13% decline in usage (Booker 1993). In New Zealand Willmott (1992) has shown public libraries to be:

> . . . very price sensitive and the imposition of charges for member-ship/loan/reference services has resulted in an immediate and drastic decline in the use of services [and] that where direct charges for public library service have been lifted, growth in the use of services has increased just as dramatically.

Comedia (*Borrowed time?* 1993) also made the point that a charged system of cultural provision 'often ends up with a narrow coterie audience'. Further evidence of the depressing power of fees on libraries, albeit in reverse, can be seen from the Channel Islands and the case of Guille-AAlles, a fee-supported library. There, use had been declining through lack of resources and the library was not gaining enough money from fees to improve the service in order to attract new members. This was changed when the library became state run and free at the point of use. There were dramatic results in terms of admission, with member-ship increasing from 2000 in 1979 to 15,000 in 1982 (Stevens 1984).

In the UK the introduction of admission charges for leisure facilities which had previously been free has resulted in a significant drop in the number of users. For instance, the number of people visiting the Science Museum almost halved between 1988 and 1990 (charges were introduced in 1989), and the Natural History Museum, which received 2.7 million visitors in 1986, saw 1991 admissions drop to 1.6 million following the introduction of charges in 1987 (*Social trends* 1993).

As the above indicates, there has been a great deal of work concerning the funding of public libraries. Research has ranged widely as academics and practitioners have sought new insights into the troubled question of finance for public library services. In the end, most who have studied the issue have concluded that public libraries should be funded substantially from the public purse.

In an information age there should be no specific limits to the precise areas for which public funding should be available. The functions of the public library are broad and potentially all-embracing. Indeed, the law demands that they be so. The demands of users and potential users require an enhancement of existing services and considerable developments in new areas. For instance, the real and reasonable demands of people with disabilities for library and information services that they can access should be properly supported from public funds. The involvement of public libraries in the exploitation of the IT superhighway will need extensive investment in equipment, cabling and operating costs. The returns for the nation on that kind of investment could be considerable, both economically and culturally. Overall, the investment of public money in public libraries achieves a return, and a range of objectives unmatched by almost any other public or private institution.

Although the case for public funding is overwhelming, there is an argument for public libraries to engage in partnerships with other organizations, voluntary bodies and private companies that could assist in developing the fiscal base of the service. According to the government:

> Individuals, firms and institutions each have a stake in improving the compet-
> itive position of their locality. The government seeks to encourage these dif-
> ferent interests to work together, so that available resources – from the private,
> voluntary and public sectors- can be brought together effectively (DTI 1996).

In terms of partnership, district councils currently own land that could interest property developers. Public library services need to be in close contact with dis-trict councils to ensure that the importance of any proposed development is eval-uated from the perspective of enhancing library provision.

Such partnerships, as Figure 7.1 illustrates, have increased over recent years, with just over three-quarters of the respondents to the present study noting that the number of such arrangements had grown in the past five years.

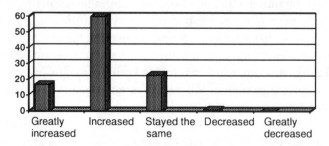

Fig. 7.1   *Partnerships with private sector organizations*

Despite such activities, the public library service budget in many local authori-ties has been greatly eroded by direct or indirect cuts. Materials' funds have suf-fered and staffing budget cuts have reduced the number of people delivering the service. This has resulted in closures and a reduction of opening hours. In addi-tion, furniture and equipment budgets have been shrunk and training budgets severely trimmed. Significantly, in the midst of the information society growth has not been available for IT and other service development.

Many librarians, in their evidence to the DNH team, argued that local author-ity politicians have found it easier to make cuts in the public library service rather than be seen to attack higher-profile and apparently more politically sensitive services. Some also suggested that, in order to protect public library budgets, there should be either a library standard spending assessment (SSA) or earmarked funding. For differing reasons the Aslib team did not accept either of these ideas.

SSAs were devised as a grant distribution mechanism and are a crude rationalization of grant allocation across different types of local authority. SSAs indicate a rough, mean and supposedly comparable cost of service provision across a range of authorities (which by and large are not comparable). It was never intended that SSAs should identify what an authority should spend on a service. In practice, however, this has been the result. The Association of Metropolitan Authorities (AMA) has carried out detailed research into the effects of applying an SSA for leisure services. Its work clearly demonstrates that public libraries would not benefit from such an arrangement. Similarly, the DNH research supported the AMA view that an SSA for public libraries would produce a random system of winners and losers that might well result in a reduction rather than improvement in the quality of public libraries.

The DNH review also rejected the idea of earmarked funding. Police services, probation services and magistrates' courts are good examples of public services that receive earmarked funding. The funding is certainly service specific and there is no room for local authorities to vary the amount of expenditure, but it was felt that such an arrangement in effect becomes a matter of ministerial in-fighting in the budget process. As a result there is a tendency for earmarked funding to become a target for top slicing at a national instead of a local level. The effect at a local level is to lose freedom and discretion in supporting and organizing services. Ultimately, services may end up being removed from local authority control as has been demonstrated by the case of the new police authorities. It is clear from the DNH and other research that users and non-users alike want public libraries to be under local, democratic control. Earmarked funding could lead to public libraries being financed and administered centrally, and this would run contrary to this public wish. For this reason, the Aslib report did not suggest that the arrangement be extended to public libraries.

There are four fundamentals of revenue budgets which are common to all library authorities. These are employees, materials, premises and IT. Such costs can only be realistically met out of what is broadly defined as taxation. However, by exploring further, and indeed publicizing widely, the beneficial effect of a public library in the local and national economy, it may be possible to obtain direct and indirect support from the businesses whose growth is helped by the near vicinity of a service point.

Evidence submitted to the DNH review and data from other sources indicate that much more work needs to be undertaken in assessing public libraries' contribution to the local economy. Buckinghamshire County Council, for instance, in a response to the DNH draft report, stated that:

> The commercial sector is becoming more aware of the importance of strategically located public libraries, because of the numbers of people who use these facilities. Over 6 million visits were made to libraries in Buckinghamshire during 1993/94 and the capital constraints currently preventing the provision of branch libraries on the flanks of the developing town of Milton Keynes is causing some concern to other retail outlets as surrounding sites are being developed.

A small project undertaken for the Yorkshire and Humberside Branch of the Library Association (Pritchard & Usherwood 1989) has shown that public libraries spend large amounts in the private sector, and that they help to support employment in private companies. In addition to this direct expenditure, every one of the respondents to that piece of research:

> . . . librarians and private sector representatives alike – considered that libraries do contribute in various ways. Contributions mentioned ranged from suggestions that a good library service adds to the cultural life of the area, thus helping to attract new business and talented individuals, to the knowledge that libraries can help 'promote' the purchase of private goods and services.

Moreover, all the respondents from private companies 'said that library cutbacks had affected their business'. Public libraries are, then, important economic organizations in their own right, and this needs to be remembered by those taking decisions about their future.

In terms of capital expenditure there is currently considerable concern over the condition of existing library buildings and the lack of investment in new libraries. In giving evidence to the public library review many respondents drew attention to what one described as 'the crying need for capital investment in the infrastructure of public libraries, particularly in buildings and facilities which are all too frequently old, shabby, difficult to manage and in the wrong location'.

There are some notable exceptions to this general rule, but it is apparent that insufficient capital is being spent on building new libraries and on the upkeep of existing ones. Under proposed government rules, no capital funding will be made available to local authorities unless finance for individual schemes has been sought from the private sector under a partnership agreement. It is argued by some that such a policy offers opportunities for public libraries. It might, for instance, be demonstrated that shopping malls and other developments are improved by the inclusion of a public library. The public library brings more people to a conventional city centre, and also contributes to an improvement in neighbouring property values. Capital programmes which involve developing or regenerating shopping areas by including a new or refurbished library may attract private sector funding support. Similarly public library services could also participate in housing development schemes in rural areas.

Recently, the government has announced that local councils will be able to make use of private sector finance in upgrading libraries, leisure centres, theatres and a number of other local facilities under the auspices of the Private Finance Initiative (PFI). It has to be said that, despite considerable government hype, this scheme has not been a great success in other areas. To quote Barnett (1996), 'there is a lingering feeling that the government's sorcery has been no more than a conjuring trick. Badly needed public projects have just stagnated in ministers' pending trays.' The PFI has also been strongly criticized by the private sector in the shape of the Building Employers' Confederation.

In addition there is considerable concern among local authorities that the government sees the PFI as a substitute for local authority funding. As Will Hutton (1996a) has observed:

> The PFI . . . is a Trojan horse undercutting the very principle of public provision in the common interest. Providers of private finance are not Santa Claus; they seek high returns on their investment and minimal risk. In order to provide the necessary returns, the public sector has to structure its activity so that cash changes hands. At best that implies building a system of market exchanges where none has existed before; at worst it means attempting to introduce charging in areas where previously it has been recognized that the benefits of public goods . . . cannot be captured through the price mechanism alone.

Sponsorship has also been advocated as an alternative source of funding, but this has serious limitations. As one respondent told the team working on the public library review:

> The funding of mobile libraries or similar services cannot be sustained by sponsorship or other forms of short-term contributions. Mobile libraries are a vital social and informational link for rural communities and must not be put at risk by speculative ventures into alternative funding.

The same argument could and should be made for the whole library service. There are also other dangers, and public librarians, like others in the public sector, should be aware of the strings attached to the gifts that sponsors bring. In another part of the communications world Potter (1993) notes how:

> At the time Rupert Murdoch was anxiously trying to gild if not renovate his image . . . he announced that his main company was going to fund a new Chair at Oxford University to the tune of £3 million. It was to be called – I do

beg your pardon, but I cannot keep a straight face – it was to be called the Murdoch Chair in Language and Communication (Potter 1993).

One wonders whether public librarians had similar qualms when 'that daily stink they call the *Sun*' (Potter 1993) sponsored children's reading activities.

To sum up, research demonstrates overwhelming public support for publicly funded libraries. The DNH study has identified some possible areas of alternative financing opportunities for public libraries. It has also examined and found wanting other possibilities. However, its main recommendation – preserving and extending when possible a public library service free at the point of use – was firmly based on the results of research into the views of users and non-users, professionals and politicians. This showed a clear preference for public libraries to be under local, democratic control. Moreover, there was some indication that the public would be willing to pay more in taxation for public library services. *British attitudes: the 11th Report of Social and Community Planning Research* also reveals that many taxpayers are willing to increase their tax commitment for particular, identified services. This view was also supported by a public consultation exercise carried out for Waverley Borough Council (1996).

As the 1992 general election demonstrated, such research findings are not always translated into votes at the ballot box, but we must hope and believe that the selfishness that influenced so many of the electorate at that time is a thing of the past. According to a number of commentators :

> . . . the tide of public opinion is now turning back towards the collectivist visions of Titmuss, Abel Smith and Townsend on grounds of both social justice and efficiency (Page 1996).

If the public are prepared to contribute extra for the public library through the council tax, then local authorities should be able to raise the charge appropriately. As part of the same process capping should be abolished and business rates should be returned to the local authority. Extensive research, opinion surveys and anecdotal evidence have all shown that public libraries are a significant public service that require adequate public funding to meet present demand and the challenges of an information-oriented future. It is difficult, however, to see how that funding can be provided under the financial restrictions currently applied to local government.

It has also been shown that the public library can make an important contribution to the local and national economy. The majority of users, politicians and professionals are against the introduction of direct charges for public library services. The principle of free and equal access to information, works of imagination and ideas is rightly embodied in most contemporary statements of public library purpose, and this is reinforced and justified by the findings of the DNH review. Admittedly, the rationale of charging for the loan of audio and video materials and not for books is difficult to explain. This point has been recognized, but given the number of library authorities making such charges it would probably have been unrealistic for the Aslib team to suggest their abolition, at least in the short term. However, it should be emphasized that the review did recommend that the principle of free and equal access to library materials and services should be extended when conditions allow. Public library managers should actively seek to create such conditions.

In the end, the financing of public libraries is a matter of political preference. As such it is a question of the public's voice as much as the individual's choice. This means that the financing of public libraries has to be managed in a way that is distinctive from that used in private companies. However, collective provision need not, as the New Right seeks to argue, result in the erosion of choice. Perhaps of all the public services public libraries most demonstrate this. Indeed, they provide far greater choice than any possible private sector alternative, as any comparison of the stock of a public library with that of even the largest bookshop will confirm. Moreover, they provide a choice that is affordable for all. There seems little doubt that the prevailing collective voice calls for the core public library services to be provided free of a direct charge on the user. This reflects the fact that for many people there is no other realistic choice.

Chapter 8

The tender trap

IN HIS LATEST book Richard Hoggart (1995b) takes his readers back to the early days of the Thatcher administration. At that time:

> . . . a joke was going round Whitehall. A head-in-the-clouds . . . idealist approached the Department of Education with a bright idea. Why not a warm open room in each city and town, fill it with books, provide tables and chairs, and also let the books be taken out on loan, and without payment? The Secretary of State was appalled: 'But such an Executive Agency would have to be cost effective. So how on earth could we make it a free service, and why should we anyway?' The joke was fulfilled in real life. By 1994 a Commission set up by the Department of National Heritage was considering the contracting out of libraries to the private sector. One hundred and forty years on and straight into reverse gear.

Many in the public library world breathed a sigh of relief when the KPMG report on contracting out concluded that 'it would be inappropriate to apply a compulsory process of tendering to the service' (KPMG 1995). The most recent government statement available at the time of writing also maintains that the National Heritage Secretary has 'ruled out – *for the present* – introducing compulsory competitive tendering in the public library service' (emphasis added). However, other noises coming from the government suggest that the minister rejects many of the arguments put by the consultants and the library profession, and favours overt competition among library authorities while they covertly cooperate. The health service is said to provide the model for this process. In addition, the Environment Minister, Sir Paul Beresford, has indicated that the government intends to impose rigorous policing of white-collar CCT and, in a recent letter to local authorities, he appeared to take the side of private sector companies who had been beaten by in-house teams in the early rounds of white-collar competition. So, although it is possible that full-blooded CCT for libraries will be put on the back burner in a pre-election period, it is unlikely to go away and could well return with a further Conservative administration.

If it were to be introduced the government would 'be seen very strongly to be ideologically driven, flying in the face of its own consultants' (McNicol 1995). Moreover, it would certainly not be reflecting the wishes of what ministers would no doubt refer to as the 'customers' of the library service. The KPMG consultation document (KPMG Peat Marwick 1994) acknowledged that 'customer reaction as to how the service is provided (either internally or externally) is a very important factor' when considering the desirability of contracting out services. From the perspective of customer reaction it is difficult to see any justification for the compulsory tendering of library services. It is clear from the Aslib research that the vast majority of both users and non-users of the service want local councils to control and run public libraries.

In the postal survey and home interviews carried out for the DNH study, people were asked which one of a number of organizations should be responsible for providing the public library service. The results show that a large majority of the population are strongly in favour of the local council carrying out this activity. The comments received by the DNH consultants also demonstrated a considerable antipathy to the prospect of businesses running libraries. There was a considerable degree of scepticism about the whole idea, with respondents fearing the introduction of charges and a lowering of standards. Such results are further supported by research into the views of professionals (Eastell 1994), politicians (Usherwood 1993a) and local surveys of public opinion.

Staffordshire, for instance, told Aslib that 'comments . . . received by telephone and passed on to staff etc. indicate strong support for the library service to be run by the local authority and to be funded from public money'. Members of the [public library] Quality Forum welcomed the emphasis on the principle of local democratic control of public libraries in the Aslib draft report, and Cornwall County Council was 'not in favour of any form of commercial input into the public library service'.

One personal respondent to the Aslib survey summarized the views of many who made submissions when he wrote:

To entrust the running of public libraries to businesses would be:-

(a) to threaten the public perception of the library as a neutral information provider;

(b) to endanger the cooperation between libraries which . . . allows the local library to serve as a gateway to resources far greater than any single library authority could provide.

Similarly strong opinions were contained in the many individual letters sent to the Aslib team. The following are typical of those received on the subject:

I totally abhor the idea of our public libraries being run by businesses. Public libraries are a national asset and should remain under the democratic control of local councils. (Member of the public)

I strongly believe that it is in the public interest to keep the library service a public service, where profit is not the ultimate issue, and where the benefit to the general public is of prime concern. (Member of the public)

The essential characteristic of a public library is that it should be publicly owned and managed as a community service for the benefit of the local inhabitants, not run by anonymous businesses interested only in how much profit they can make. Over the past ten years, as a result of continued squeezing of local authorities' budgets, the library services have been cut again and again, but local authorities at least appreciate what the local community requires and can match the service they provide to the needs of the people in the community. (Husband and wife))

What I think would be the death of the public library service as we know it would be for a business concern (for example, one with interests in publishing and the wholesale/retail book trade with experience of library supply) being awarded a contract for the provision of public library services. My concern is informed partly by my impression of the service quality of the mainstream library supply companies, and partly by the experience of seeing the effect on service delivery and costs of public utilities since privatization. Although a degree of public accountability is maintained by the regulatory bodies such as Oftel and Ofwat, that control is at one remove from the supplier, and often exercised against the supplier's interests. The public interest has to be played off against that of the shareholders. We must learn from that experience. (Member of the public)

The last point is echoed by Hoggart (1995b), who writes:

Unless corralled by legislation the commercial contractors will do according to their nature. Their early morning hymn is . . . 'My first duty is to my shareholders'. That recurrent phrase – particularly repellent when it refers to . . . a public service – is presumed to solve and absolve all.

The cant phrases that may accompany this kind of activity have been beautifully caught in the recent BBC radio series 'Mammon'. The title says it all.

The evidence clearly suggests that there would be little or no support for any change in legislation to allow private companies to run library services. The research carried out for the DNH, and other studies, shows little public, professional or political support for the contracting out of library services. It is therefore not surprising that Aslib recommended that public library services should be run and controlled by democratically elected local councils. To force local councils to contract out services would be to ignore public opinion and an offence against local choice.

Most of the senior library managers responding to the questionnaire sent out as part of the preparation for this book were also against the idea. Their arguments were professional, practical and pragmatic. They felt that:

> Competitive tendering has been ideologically led. There is little evidence that it improves quality. However, the management processes involved can be beneficial if introduced selectively. They can be applied informally rather than constructed so as to prepare for competition. The process of going out to competition other than for some non-core activities appears to be time consuming, and costly and unproven. The minimalist pilot projects for the KPMG study appear to have been largely fruitless. (English metropolitan district)

Another, speaking from experience, said:

> I do not believe that competitive tendering has any significant role in the public library service, because there is no external market, there are considerable difficulties in drawing up realistic specifications for complex educational institutions, and the flexibility to respond to changing circumstances would be curtailed. I am a great believer in cost effectiveness and efficiency, but I remain to be convinced that this would be a way forward for libraries. The proposal to hive off areas of work for compulsory competitive tendering, such as media, mobile libraries etc., I feel would create more confusion and difficulty than would be outweighed by any possible benefits. Various services in the libraries, such as cleaning and catering, have been awarded to outside contractors, but the results do not seem to have been particularly beneficial in terms of service or cost effectiveness, and in some areas have resulted in positive deterioration. (English metropolitan district)

Others were of the opinion that:

> CCT has no place in the public library service. There are possibilities for VCT or contracting out but direct service provision is best done by the employees of the council, available to elected members and free from 'commercial' pressures. (English county)

> The public library service should be just that and not run by organizations looking to make a profit from a service that is the bedrock of opportunity for all citizens. (English county)

> I do not believe that CT for public libraries is desirable. I do not believe that there is private sector expertise to deliver a high quality service. Although the

public library service may have much to learn from the private sector the success depends upon a professional understanding and professional rigour
which does not exist in the private sector. (Scottish district)

Many regarded the contracting out process as little more than an expensive way
of introducing sound management techniques. In the words of one respondent,
'the Brent exercise only proved that if proper management methods had been in
place beforehand the benefits would have been negligible' (Welsh District).
Similarly, a London respondent felt that 'the benefits of competitive tendering
can all be achieved without going down the contract route. The potential benefits
of it are yet to be proven' (London borough). For another librarian CCT was 'a
distraction from service delivery *but* if a quasi market is used [there is] potential
for adopting good management practices. Costs too much, saves too little'
(English metropolitan district). Another found 'the *process* of client/contractor
[unclear word] (i.e. specifying, monitoring and evaluating) . . . beneficial to the
service as a kind of quality raising and bench marking. It is an effective way of
managing. [but] The further *tendering* process . . . an expensive and time wasting
irrelevance'. (London borough)

The government, as is clear from its response to the KPMG study, is still
propagating the view that good management practices are to be equated with
those used in the private sector. A letter to chief librarians from the DNH suggested that 'there would be considerable benefits to be gained from the application of commercial management techniques to many aspects of libraries'. In fact,
the KPMG report does not mention commercial management techniques but
refers to management techniques used 'by other public services and indeed, in
some public library authorities themselves;.

There are many disadvantages with the CCT process. A large number of
respondents to the present study commented that 'CT will fragment the library
service, break up existing partnerships, collaborative agreements and inter- and
intralibrary cooperation' (London borough). Without doubt CCT will have an
adverse effect on local, regional and national library networks. As the Library
Association stated, 'it is precisely because . . . libraries in a system act as a network, each contributing to the overall strength of the network, that it is dangerous to split such services up to be put out to competitive tendering' (Library
Association 1991). All kinds of cooperative arrangements, such as cooperative
training, staffing arrangements and the development of specialist collections,
could be put at risk.

There must also be concerns for specialist staff. One of the library authorities
visited by Eastell (1994) had already lost specialist posts as the result of the
client/contractor split. There are particular concerns over the future of community librarians and those serving minority ethnic groups. Such posts may be put
at risk because of changes in the criteria for Section 11 funding and the imple-

mentation of Compulsory Competitive Tendering (Kendall, 1992). As one respondent told Eastell, 'in a contracted situation . . . expertise does not readily fit within the contractor side. There is a bit of both – a bit of service delivery and a bit of service monitoring and development . . . Those posts could be the ones at risk.'

In one authority it was already found 'much more difficult to work with other . . . departments now they have been contracted out. Such departments are now customer driven – if indeed I am a customer' (London borough). Many respondents to Eastell's (1994) study felt that competitive tendering would see the demise of the 'open door' policy, which enables people from neighbouring authorities to use the libraries of another authority, usually free of charge. This, they felt, would be replaced by some form of charging, either directly to the user or to the local authority.

The public and private sectors have different attitudes to cooperation and competition. Cooperation is rarely part of the private sector culture whereas 'librarians have a predisposition towards cooperation. Put two librarians in a room and they'll come up with a cooperative plan.' (Chief librarian, quoted in Eastell 1994). Indeed one of the great strengths of British librarianship has been the ability of diverse parts of the service to cooperate. It would be a great pity if the opportunities of cooperation were to be sacrificed on the altar of competition. In such a scenario the interdependence of library services would be seriously challenged by the fragmentation that would result from commercial rivalry.

One respondent, despite having 'no objections in principle [could] see practical disadvantages for the user as . . . CT can lead to less flexibility once a contract has been agreed, even if there is an ability to vary the contract' (London borough). Indeed, many have questioned the practicality of developing a service specification that would be flexible and responsive to the changing needs of library communities. For example Heinitz (1993) told a public libraries conference:

> The running of a comprehensive and efficient library service must mean flexibility and adaptability. Adaptability to the changing needs and aspiration of the community. Try writing that into a specification for CCT.

A librarian responding to the present study is of the opinion that 'it is perfectly possible for an organization to be clear about its objectives and strategies without having to write a specification for every element of work' (English county).

Although many would, no doubt, argue that it is the role of the library manager to draw up an adequate specification, the difficulties of specifying the intangibles of a public library service are not to be underestimated. It is far from easy to specify the values that underpin the public library service in such a way that they will be reflected fully in what a contractor provides.

Those involved with Eastell's (1994) study even reported difficulties in dealing with more tangible outcomes:

> For example in cleaning, silly things like they [the contractor] wouldn't move chairs out from the table because that wasn't specified.

Moreover, the important human factor, which is a fundamental aspect of many public library services, may indeed be contracted out if experience in other fields is anything to go by. For instance, Elcock (1996) describes how:

> The problems inherent in competitive tendering became apparent when Wandsworth Borough Council, which had tendered out residential care for its old people, discovered that the meal portions served at the privately run old people's homes had been reduced to starvation levels to protect the company's profit margins (Elcock 1996).

With just a few exceptions, respondents to the present study were against CCT for core services. When asked to consider the limits of competitive tendering for the public library services, most respondents felt that there were 'theoretically none [but] in practice support services such as building maintenance, book processing, vehicle servicing etc.' (Northern Ireland Library and Education Board) were all that should be considered. Similarly, another respondent would limit contracting to:

> ... furniture and equipment supplies, building contracts, centralized cataloguing services, supply of vehicles. Franchising of videos, provision of bookshops and other non-core services on library premises. Wouldn't go much beyond this – certainly not as far as direct provision of the core library service. (Northern Ireland Library and Education Board)

In another authority, CT:

> ... has proved capable of reducing costs in some areas of subsidiary services, e.g. cleaning, but the size of the operation governs the amount of savings which can be achieved. In my own authority the possible savings would, I believe, be outweighed by the cost of the process. (Welsh county)

A minority of respondents to the present study were more favourably inclined to the concept. One felt that:

> Ultimately, pressure for contracting for public services will be difficult to resist [and that] there is no limit, [to CCT], but at present a limited market. The domino effect is likely over time as individual authorities take a contracting route, others will follow. Some parts of the service will go out first, most

obviously FM of computer services. Library (book) supply will be an increasingly likely candidate. (English county)

Three respondents were critical of what they perceived to be the profession's stance on the subject. One argued:

It is for authorities to determine a specification with appropriate standards. This can be tested against potential providers. Only the evaluation of approaches or bids can determine whether there is any merit or effective market. There is no obligation to accept bids which fail to meet quality thresholds. If current providers feel they are so good, what have they got to lose by being assessed against the market place? (London borough)

Another argued that:

. . . competitive tendering *could* be a viable option for *some* library services in a certain context. I don't think it is something that would universally provide a solution, but neither do I think that it is *necessarily* the bête noire it is considered to be by most of the profession. (London borough, original emphasis)

For another:

. . . a growing market is emerging which means many library professionals will have to be less naive than they are now. Staffing is always the highest overhead in our service and will always be undercut by the private sector. (English county)

For the majority, however, the idea of CCT was either 'completely irrelevant' (English county) or:

. . . a waste of resources for public libraries. Resources are scarce enough without having to resort to further non-library usage of staff time and expertise to satisfy a policy of government which has no basis in reality. (Scottish district)

Another respondent asked with some force that 'we please stop wasting time and money and address the real issues (English metropolitan district). Although it did not put the argument in such strong terms, the KPMG report also questioned the costs of contracting out, particularly in relatively small library authorities.

More generally:

The contract principle is having its own domino effect. There is an explosion of market transactions that must be written down, monitored and audited: this inevitably involves an inflation of management costs. (Hutton 1996b)

There are also a number of less obvious costs. Any true evaluation of contracting out also needs to take account of the costs of unemployment that often results from the process. To quote from the government itself, 'Since 1979 the number of public sector employees has fallen from 7.4 million to 5.3 million' (DTI 1996). Ironically, in the same paragraph as those figures there is a homily about the need to raise the standards of essential services. Other research (Clouston 1991; White & Hutchinson 1996) has demonstrated the adverse effect of CCT on the pay and conditions of local government workers.

There is also a democratic price to be paid. With CCT it is much more diffi-cult for local elected members to deal with complaints from members of the public. In addition, a council of one colour may be tied to a contract undertaken by a previous administration of a different political persuasion. The democratic process allows for public accountability and provides the necessary checks and balances to protect the citizen, rather than cheques and balances for the benefit of shareholders in private companies.

This is not to say that the private sector should not be involved with the pub-lic library service in any way. As the DNH review showed, little would be gained and much lost if businesses were to run public libraries, but there could be opportunities for cooperative programmes involving partnerships with the pri-vate and voluntary sectors. In the words of one respondent:

> CCT is totally inappropriate. Partnership is the key and the ability to choose the most efficient and effective method of service testing which may include market testing. (English county)

Some of these arrangements might be quite different in shape and function from what has gone before. References in the literature to concepts such as 'the bor-derless library' suggest that it is, or soon will be, possible to share information in digital form on a network. Such a network will be capable of generating new forms of service and cooperation.

Partnerships and cooperative arrangements are one thing but, as we have seen, there is considerable evidence to show that public and professional opinion is against the commercialization of public services. Data from one of the most recent surveys (*The glue that binds* 1996) show that:

> . . . 77% believe public services should be under public control; and as many as 61% believe they should be owned by the state. Eighty percent believe too many public services have been privatized. There is no difference in the pre-dominant views across the social classes or across political parties.

Semantic differences notwithstanding, the compulsory contracting out of public library services is rightly perceived to be a privatization too far.

Chapter 9

Taking stock

IN DAYS GONE by The Library Association used to set an examination question asking, in effect, whether a librarian should be a manager or a book person. However, in the more recent past it has seemed that books and other library material have been hardly considered, save perhaps as a way of boosting issues or cutting costs. As Labdon (1991) observed, 'As a specialism, the art of selecting novels for adults is virtually dead in public libraries'. A respondent to the Sheffield/Loughborough project on TQM, when asked if QM had had an impact on candidates selected for employment, replied, 'we have moved away from requiring any knowledge of books for one thing'. At the same time politicians have asked, 'what purpose does reading serve and why should it be provided free of a direct charge on the user?' (cf Sproat 1993).

Moreover, as the impact of the new managerialism and the associated political imperatives led to the commercialization of library services, there was, as Hoggart (1995b) among others, noted:

> . . . pressure on public libraries to reduce both their opening hours and their buying across a wide range of tastes and levels; they then focus their buying on the already popular.

The result of all this was to be seen in library stocks which announced that librarians were more concerned with the quantity of issues likely to be achieved by a particular item, rather than the quality of the material on offer. Thus a researcher looking at Brent, an authority which has enthusiastically embraced the new management orthodoxies, was told by:

> . . . a senior librarian . . . that the average Mills and Boon reader was still well served but that [a] student needing the latest publication in their subject area would be very unlikely to find such material (Walker, G. 1994).

The content of library materials, particularly imaginative literature, has been seen as an adjunct to public library management rather than as an integral part of the process. With notable exceptions, such as Margaret Kinnell's (1991) collection on *Managing fiction in libraries*, it has not been a major concern of writers contributing to the more recent professional literature. However, we make no apologies for including it here for, as the DNH review and much previous research has shown, reading is still an important aspect of the modern public library service. Any meaningful rediscovery of public library management must include some reference to stock management, selection and development. It is a function that 'places tremendous demands on the library manager. Managing the fiction service effectively is the most visible sign to a critical public of the success of a library' (Kinnell 1991).

There is no need to spend much time discussing the various selection practices or the various scientific methods that have been used over the years. Suffice it to say that, as the earlier quote from Alan Taylor (1993) demonstrates, there are those who are looking for a mathematically correct approach and seek to place the emphasis on 'books and quantification' in order to overcome 'a general lack of meaningful and sophisticated quantification in our management of resources' (Betts, 1985).

Mathematics aside, it is rare to see any professional discussion of the criteria that should be used by librarians when selecting materials for public library collections. Works of imagination, as we shall see, present some special difficulties, but general selection criteria should include some consideration of the authority of a work, its scope, the treatment of the subject, the arrangement of the material, and the format in which it is presented. In addition, there may be special factors arising from the nature and location of the library community to be served.

In considering the authority of a work it is necessary to ask questions such as What do we know about the author? What are her or his qualifications for writing on this particular topic? What is known about the publisher and what is their reputation in the field? One should, for instance, be mildly suspicious of a Mills and Boon publication on nuclear physics! It is also necessary to ascertain whether the book is based on a previous edition, and if so, what is known about the use made of that. Indeed, is it really a new edition?

Selectors also need to consider the scope of the work. What is its stated purpose and is it made clear? How up to date is it? How good is the bibliography? Does the book guide the user to any additional sources of information or ideas? What is the date of the latest reference? It is also important to assess the accuracy of the information given and to check for any hidden bias, and to ascertain the style and level of approach to the subject. In this regard selectors should be concerned with such matters as the quality of the index and the sequence of arrangement.

In considering the physical format of an item it is necessary to have regard for the quality of the illustrations. Are they justified, in all senses of the word, and how recent are they? One might also need to judge the suitability of the format for a public lending collection.

All these are perhaps the kind of features that one would consider in review-ing a book, but in selecting an item for a particular public library other factors also need to be taken into account. Because of the volume of material available and the limitations of finance, not to say space, a public library needs to have a selection policy that reflects the interests of the community and meets commu-nity and individual needs. This will help selectors decide whether the money spent on a particular item is being well spent. In considering that question it is necessary to think about the long-term as well as the short-term answer.

The librarian needs to consider how well an item fits in with the arrangement and subject coverage of the current library stock. Would it be more appropriate for other libraries in the locality, and/or is it the kind of material that might be left to interlibrary loans or other cooperative arrangements? In answering such questions it is necessary to be aware that the current cost of an interlibrary loan, excluding staff costs, is around £6 Sometimes, of course, a service may wish to acquire an item because it has a particular local connection by way of author or subject.

The librarian will need to assess the current – and likely future – demand for an item. There are certain clues to this such as the amount of publicity a publica-tion has received and the type of reviews it has had. Current events, the level of reservations and past demand for books by a particular author, or on a particular subject, are also indicators that can be used. It is important, however, to distin-guish between true and artificial demands, which are sometimes created by pres-sure groups. In addition, as will be discussed later, public libraries, as a public service, must not fall into the trap of being entirely demand led.

Librarians also need to take account of the wider society in which they live and work, and beware of racial, gender and other forms of stereotyping. This leads to an area of discussion that could be the subject of a separate book, and suffice it to say that the debate continues. It is an area where the rhetoric of pro-fessional statements and the reality of stock selection are not always at one (Cole & Usherwood, in press).

The evaluation and selection of fiction can present public librarians with spe-cial problems. Novelists portray an imaginative view of life, and the serious nov-elist may frequently take as a theme a topic which is not conventional, and use controversial approaches. A number of American libraries have set out what they term 'appropriate criteria' with regard to the selection of fiction but, with the always important exception of those who work with children, the British library profession has, of late, not been overconcerned with such matters.

A charter for public libraries, published by The Library Association in 1993, con-tained a complete section on 'Books and other stock'. The subsequent work to develop standards to support the statements made in that section presented the researchers with a number of difficulties and revealed several nettles which, even after 150 years, the profession has still failed to grasp. Librarians interviewed as part of the research on standards expressed a variety of views, as is evident from the following extracts:

> Selection should include both established and new authors. First novels are an obvious area of fiction where circulating collections may maximize both distribution and use. So we are staying within those [*A Charter* . . .] stock selection guidelines . . . ,we're not just saying 'we'll buy whatever is most popular', we're taking as a principle that we will seek to provide some copies of new material . . . . Poetry is a bit more difficult, there's never a lot of demand for poetry and I am not sure we have a commitment to new poetry but certainly new fiction, we're continuing to provide people with access to first authors. (London borough).

> We feel that part of the role of libraries is to ensure that there is a broad range of literature available, that's not to reduce it to the most popular in any community because the community doesn't know all the possible options that could be followed, and it's part of our role to assume some sort of educative aspect . . . and it would be . . . a denial of our role to say 'well, we'll just buy what people want'. (English county)

> In the good days when money wasn't so bad, you could afford to be an idealist . . . but not these days it's much harder to do, you've got to justify a lot more. I might think buying 20 copies of Catherine Cookson was more than enough, but probably to hundreds of people out there, buying 50 copies of Catherine Cookson would *not* be enough. (English metropolitan district)

Others tended to mix idealism with the techniques used in supermarkets:

> I was talking to someone . . . about how when you go to a supermarket that there's an element of choice, where if you want to go and have fresh vegetables you can, and you can go and pick your own vegetables, and you go and weigh them, but equally on occasions . . . you want the packs . . . and I was saying, we don't do this in libraries at all we go very much for the fresh fruit. (London borough)

At some point the public librarian will be faced with the central dichotomy of value versus demand. Basically, do you give the public what they want or do you concentrate on material considered 'good'? Such arguments are brought into sharper focus at a time of declining resources. Readers will be aware of the arguments on both sides and there is no need to repeat them here. However, it appears that over the past few years a combination of market forces and a misplaced fear of elitism has meant that rather too many public librarians have been unwilling – or worse, unable – to differentiate between the good and the bad.

Although it would not be charitable to deny some access to the hundreds of people who crave Catherine Cookson, it is surely the prime role of the public library to bring people into contact with the best, and to give them the opportunity to sample that which may not be readily available elsewhere. The best will be based on a professional value judgment, and it can of course be selected from both the posh and the popular wings of our culture.

In the 1980s a combination of 'marketing speak' and inappropriate management techniques seemed to result in what might be termed the 'Ratner's school of stock management': 'We know that it is rubbish but it is what the people want' appeared to be the governing philosophy. However, to paraphrase the dramatist Arnold Wesker, public librarians should not just give people what they want, because they deserve better than that. Indeed, there is the very real danger that in giving people what we think they want we will patronize our users. In 1995 there were some very interesting pieces on this theme in the British press. As it happens, these were written in light of a report on the BBC, but their conclusions are relevant to libraries.

As part of this debate Richard Hoggart (1995a) asked, 'Why treat us like dimwits? He went on to talk about the 'shifting about with the meaning of quality', saying that it led to:

> . . . nervous and excessive praise for the taste of the people out there. Some of us have been saying for years that we . . . are not as daft as those who seek our support often seem to assume.

He went on to say:

> Many people are only basically and not critically literate. That goes partly with our divisive education system. More importantly, it is sustained by those vast engines of persuasion which, in their own interest, tell us that we need not lift our eyes higher or wider, that their trash is good bread . . . . For all of us the appetite grows by what it feeds on: it is easier to reinforce existing low taste than to suggest that the world is wider and deeper.

Like the BBC, public libraries can show that the world is wider and deeper, but they will not achieve this if they engage in a populist chase to maximize issues. There have been some vigorous debates on this topic in the United States, which have been concerned with the demand-driven approach adopted by Baltimore County Library (see Rawlinson 1981, 1986). In the more recent past, at least one British public library, in its charter statement, promised to supply the top 20 books to its 'customers'. This was rather like setting the quality of British television by reference to the top 20 programmes. It is the kind of policy that perpetuates 'The Generation Game' and axes 'The Late Show'.

There is a lesson here for the library world as it is encouraged to become more commercialized, responding to wants rather than needs. The public library, if it is to survive and remain true to its public purpose, will need to protect and promote good literature, first novelists and poetry. Although it is not perfect, *A charter for public libraries* encourages library authorities to do this, and rightly so. We must not treat our users as if they all had the intellectual aspirations of Julie Burchill. We should encourage them to experiment and try a different and perhaps more difficult reading experience. Sad to say, however, in our present climate, 'difficulty is not seen as a challenge but as a justificatioii for avoidance. The result is a society which is increasingly obsessed with instant gratification, undemanding comforts and off-the-shelf satisfactions' (Naughton (1995).

Thus, in an increasingly commercial book trade, the intelligent authors who sell less are in danger of being dropped as publishers' resources are directed towards genre or potboiling writers. The consumerist-cum-managerialist perspective has led to a situation in which 'some publishers are even considering the sending out of manuscripts to focus groups' (Lawson 1996). In such circumstances public libraries have an even greater responsibility to provide and promote good literature. They should seek to influence rather than slavishly follow public taste. Unless they are willing to take on this responsibility, public librarians may be faced with the reality of Derek Law's (1996) bizarre but stark image of:

> . . . the public library couch potato, relegated- in a horrible parody of *Brave new world* – to supplying Jeffrey Archer novels to the population in order to keep it in a semi-comatose state.

Public librarians must be prepared, in all senses of the word, to select material on the basis of professional judgment rather than some dubious marketing activity. As Lawson (1996) has written:

> Many considerable works of art, in all genres, have led rather than followed taste. A focus group would almost have forced radical restructuring of *Citizen Kane*, while no scratch cards would have asked for *Look back in anger*, and no audience research questionnaires would have indicated that an innovative sitcom such as 'One Foot in the Grave' was capable of gaining 15 million viewers. The consumer may sometimes be wrong.

The public librarian must have the confidence to make judgments on the behalf of the community. If staff are to do this they will require adequate training and education in collection development and stock management. Public library managers should be encouraged – indeed required – to read literature as part of their professional development. It is beginning to happen: some library authorities are now sending their staff on literature awareness programmes. Staff at Sheffield

public library, for example, have participated in such a course. This was organized by Yorkshire and Humberside Arts and included such topics as black literature and professional responsibilities. Participants also had to discuss the novels
they had read as part of the programme.

In practice there will always be a degree of tension on the matter of value versus demand, but the flexible nature of the public library means that librarians are
in a position to reconcile the dilemma, at least to some extent. Unlike the broad-
caster who, even in these days of video and audio recorders, is trapped by schedules, the manager of a library service can physically provide a very wide range of
material at the same place and time.

When times are hard, however, priorities will have to be identified and the
public librarian must be clear as to what these are. They must avoid what
Hoggart terms 'populist relativism'. This has led librarians to say that:

> . . . they will not clutter their shelves with the 'classics'. Half a dozen of each
> Jack Higgins title and a dozen of each Barbara Cartland need the space . . . .
> Those . . . more inclined to linguistic PR produce: 'What is needed is a lean,
> muscular, light turnover stock presented in attractive and imaginative ways'.
> The more insecure take refuge in informatics, germ free in 'value' terms
> (Hoggart 1995b).

Hoggart goes on to ask, 'To what are the Schools of Librarianship introducing
their students if not, among much else, to the importance of imaginative literature?' Authors from within the profession have also complained that 'the training
and education of librarians focuses on computerized information retrieval and
information management, and leisure-related topics such as libraries and the arts,
or popular fiction and its readership, have been curtailed or marginalized to
accommodate this' (Snape 1995). There is some truth in these accusations,
although there is some recent evidence to suggest that we are moving away from
what was yet another example of the poverty of 1980s thinking. For instance, in
the 1995–6 academic year, as a result of an Arts Council report (Hicks 1995) and
subsequent financial support, the University of Central England and the
University of Sheffield introduced modules on the promotion of literature in
libraries. It should also be said that the Arts Council report does indicate a rather
higher level of activity in the LIS departments than some of the critics suggest.
Public library students at Sheffield, for instance, have for many years taken part
in a practical stock selection exercise whereby they 'select' books for local community libraries or a special service. In addition, Loughborough University has
recently been awarded a grant to investigate the promotion of literature in public
libraries.

There has also been some activity in the profession which indicates that not all public librarians are content to live with populist relativism. As Michael Ignatieff (1991) has noted:

> Promotional campaigns to get readers to try Afro-Caribbean, Latin American and Eastern European fiction have had some success in breaking the stranglehold of Barbara Cartland and Jeffrey Archer on popular literary taste.

Some librarians have quite deliberately set out to 'promote literature'. A review of some recent projects can be found in *Shelf talk* (1996). They range from promotions of books by local authors to a festival of science fiction and a project to create opportunities for people with learning difficulties to enjoy literature through reading and active participation. The projects sometimes reflect different priorities and philosophies but, in the words of the Chairperson of the Library and Information Commission, they demonstrate that 'public libraries are about reader development and creating reading opportunities' (Evans 1996a).

The political perspective, as considered in Chapter 2, also has a part to play in stock management. In the word of one committee chairperson (quoted in Usherwood 1993a), the library committee 'should have basic principles. The policy behind book buying should be thrashed out in committee.' Indeed, it was ever the way. Library historians will recall Sayers' graphic description of the elected members' involvement in stock selection and the practice of councillors approving or otherwise a list of books submitted by the librarian. Savage (1942) also devoted a whole chapter of *The librarian and his committee* to discussing the procedure. Thompson (1975) also indicated that elected members and library committees took a considerable interest – some might argue a censorious interest – in the material that public libraries should or should not provide. He concluded that:

> The vast majority of cases of attempted censorship result from the actions of council members. Although these cases include some in which councillors have acted on behalf of individual readers or groups, the vast majority show the motivation for censorship as deriving from the personal opinions and tastes of individual councillors (Thompson 1975).

Later research (Usherwood 1993a) suggested that elected members are still taking more than a passing interest in the material stocked and displayed in public libraries.

In the current political climate stock selection and related matters may have to be considered by members serving on other than library committees. Wares (1989) has described how, in Camden, the Race and Community Relations and Women's Committees, the Policy and Resources Committee and the full council, in addition to the committee responsible for the library service, asked for reports on and/or debated book selection, exhibitions, arts events and the like. The conclusion of the debate was 'that Camden Libraries would maintain their long tradition of a no cenosrship policy. Any book that is sold openly and lawfully, and for which a demand exists may be found in a Camden library.'

Whereas it would be wrong to overemphasize the degree to which elected members involve themselves in stock selection, the evidence (Usherwood 1993a) does suggest that in a significant number of cases they do influence the decisions of officers. This influence is sometimes direct but more often indirect, in that librarians are expected to be 'sensible enough not to put on anything that might upset politically or morally'. In an earlier piece of research Lomer and Rogers (1983) were able to report that 'in those rare instances where a librarian was asked to remove material, this was always considered to be unacceptable to the librarian involved. One librarian told his committee categorically that he would not.'

Such actions are still considered unacceptable by most librarians, but today categorical refusal is more likely to be replaced by advice. This was certainly the case during the News International dispute, when 'In the early part of 1986 a number of local authorities . . . instructed the libraries under their jurisdiction . . . to suspend their subscriptions to newspapers and periodicals published by News International' (Malley 1990). The dangers of not taking professional advice in such circumstances were revealed by Christine Wares, who told a Library Association audience that the only time the council 'have not listened to my advice and deliberately flouted my professional judgment they ended up in the High Court; got their decision overturned; attracted bad publicity . . . and incurred enormous costs (Wares 1989).

A Canadian researcher and observer of the British scene has considered the dilemma facing a chief librarian if the local politicians rejected a selection policy recommended by the librarian. She found that:

> It was referred to as 'the ultimate question' whether one capitulates and compromises one's professional and/or political beliefs, or whether one resigns. None of [her] respondents speculated about what their course of action would be, the dilemma was left unresolved (Curry 1993).

Such issues are likely to be emphasized by the new technology. Public library connections to the Internet, for example, will add even greater complexity to the issues of stock management and selection discussed in this chapter. Research on this topic is in progress in many places, but it is an example of an issue where, to find some of the answers, we may need to go back to our professional roots in order to rediscover a sense of direction for the future.

Part 4

Back to the future

When you vote next time, bear one simple statistic in mind. Spending on public services is at least £20 billion, or one-tenth, less than it would have been had it kept pace with the economy over the past seven years. Gradgrind rules, and it's not OK.

MICHAEL IGNATIEFF, *'Gradgrind rules in the public libraries'*, 1991

The myth has been there – and I'm guilty of having perpetrated that myth – of the virtue of boosting companies by remaking the corporate entity into a leaner, more flexible and competitive organization. This was music to the ears of investors but at the end of the day, though some of the things that were done were good, it was wrong.

If you compete by building you have a future. If you compete by cutting you don't.

STEPHEN S. ROACH (1996) A leading American management guru admits that he got it all wrong. (Carlin 1996)

Chapter 10

A crisis in public library management?

> Everyone should have an appreciation of what the profession was like when librarians confronted large issues, were unafraid of controversy, were convinced of the instrumentality of technology, were wholly absorbed in the human and social dimensions of their work, were able to rise above the mediocrity inevitably introduced by the disease of managementitis (Roberts 1994).

IN THE DREARY decade that was the 1980s we were led to believe that go-getting entrepreneurs were heroes and that professionals and bureaucrats were villains. A person's worth was, quite literally in some silly games played by city posers, judged by the amount of money they had in their wallet. The Conservative administration of that time set out to promote the ideas of individualism and the enterprise culture. It was, as Lord Young admitted in a recent television programme ('Peter York's Eighties', 1996), a quite deliberate piece of social engineering. The government expressed total confidence in business leaders. Thus in the words of John Naughton (1996):

> . . . the most insidious legacy of Thatcherism: [is] its comprehensive implementation of the proposition that the only views which matter are those of men (they are mostly men) in suits who spend their lives crawling along the 'bottom line'. Everywhere we look – broadcasting, the arts, universities, the health service, research councils, quangos of every ilk – we find courts and councils and boards of governors and trustees stuffed with accountants, company directors, management consultants and other proponents of commercial realism.

In many respects this new management culture was an attack on the rights of the independent professional. There have always been potential conflicts for professionals working in large organizations, and these have been recognized for some time in the general management literature and also in the more specialist literature of the library profession (Usherwood 1980). In recent years, however, such conflicts have increased as a result of the growing emphasis on commercial values. Such values have been reinforced through training courses and recruitment policies which, as the last chapter indicated, 'have moved away from requiring any knowledge of books'.

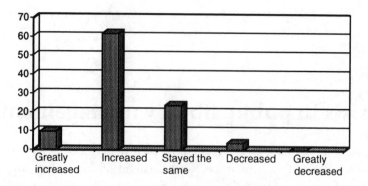

Fig. 10.1 *Emphasis on commercial values as opposed to professional values*

As Figure 10.1 shows, 72% of the respondents to the survey of chief librarians carried out for this book felt that the emphasis on commercial, as opposed to professional, values had increased or greatly increased over the past few years. This is a trend that concerns many chief librarians because, as one wrote with some feeling, it:

> . . . affects the way staff at all levels look at themselves and their job in the organization . . . They are weary of the political and financial environment in which we exist and in such circumstances recognizing and making ethical choices is extremely difficult. (English county)

Another local authority:

> . . . is going through a process of cultural change with a shift from the public to private sector values. Library staff are fearful that the whole baby, or at least [a] significant part of it, is at risk of being thrown out with the bathwater. (London borough)

A further respondent referred to 'the dilution of professional standards and ethics [and] more selfishness' (English county).

Another said that 'the major factor is finance and financial problems which push us into decisions which are funding or income based rather than stemming solely from professional judgment' (English county). In an English metropolitan district, 'commercialism has crept into the culture of the organization, with the need to increase income etc. to stave off cuts'. This has permeated 'the ethics and values of the organization, as well as in practical ways' (English metropolitan district). The professional and personal impact of this is reflected in the comment of a chief librarian, who stated that:

> The word 'ethical' is one which I have some difficulty with. The culture of the organization is concerned with the production of quality, cost-effective

services but this is more a matter of management than of professional ethics. (English county)

For another respondent:

> The potential conflict between service philosophy and commercial management has become more acute without as yet causing real problems. I feel that this conflict will increase over the next few years aided by the enforced change of local government reorganization. (Scottish district)

In 1989 Alban-Metcalf 's research identified significant differences between the attitudes to work of managers and professionals in the private sector and those in the public sector. 'It indicated that private sector managers regard factors such as high earnings and fringe benefits as more important than those in the public sector.' However, data from the survey carried out for the present work suggest that there is now a considerable split in professionals' attitudes to the change to a private sector culture in the public library service. As Figure 10.2 shows, 40% regarded it in a positive way, whereas a third perceived it as a negative development.

As Pollitt (1993) observes, workers in the public sector 'have been taught to think of themselves as managers and career rewards have begun to favour those who emphasize this dimension'. We are beginning to see the rise of a new group of workers who are less concerned with professional values than personal career advancement and progression. David Owen (1995) asks, 'should one criticize colleagues who conform to this principle by espousing market testing, the creation of business units and contracting out of services?' He responds to his own question by saying, 'Plainly, it would be unjust to denigrate their attempts to reflect the local will, but one can question the enthusiasm with which some have

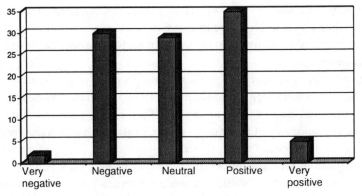

Fig. 10.2 *Attitudes to 'private sector' culture*

expounded such methods as a panacea for all of the problems the modern public library is facing'.

One can indeed, for what we are seeing, in the words of one respondent, is 'the denigration of "professionals" and the rise of the general manager' (English county). In the library world this is reflected in the view that 'questions . . . whether all *professional* library positions require a master's degree in library science or the equivalent. [and suggests that] Many of them should require master's in business administration or degrees in human resources' (St Clair 1994a, emphasis added). The more cynical reader may feel that such an opinion gives weight to the argument that MBA stands for 'mediocre but arrogant'.

Be that as it may, it does reflect a modern wisdom that a manager can undertake any professional task. The genesis of this kind of thinking can, in the words of one writer, 'be traced back to the Holy of Holies, the Harvard Business School, which has been purveying the delusion of all-round management competence for over half a century'. We must, then, be aware of what the same author has called the 'great management delusion' (Faith 1995). This is 'the widely held belief that there is such a thing as managerial competence, a pure skill that can be applied to any business sector or public organization. In the public sector, GMD has already done untold damage.' It should be noted that this view is not shared by a minority of respondents to the present study. They felt that 'the day of the "professional" specialist, e.g. the librarian or curator, is just about gone. Managers are what is needed' (Scottish regional authority).

For some, a commitment to public service and its educational and social impact are no longer satisfactory reasons for being a librarian. Indeed, the gurus tell us that 'librarians must reject absolutely and permanently their connections with education and the educational establishment' (St Clair 1994b) in order to advance their cause. This kind of argument reflects the 'Greed is Good' philosophy so prevalent during the low point of 1980s' yuppie culture, but it is unlikely to be of help to those currently working in genuine learning organizations, academic or public libraries. Nowhere in that view is there any room for public service values. Ideas of equity, justice and citizenship are seen as restraints on personal advancement.

The librarian is encouraged to be an entrepreneur yet, as Parsons (1988) points out, the entrepreneur 'exploits informational discrepancies between individual sellers and buyers. In other words, [he or she] makes profit through exploiting the ignorance of other traders.' It is an approach that is the very opposite of the public librarian's professional commitment to counter ignorance and the inequalities in access to information. Unfortunately, such behaviour is not unknown in today's library world: witness the librarian who built a whole paper around the fact that his music librarian had sold records in a library sale for more than he had paid for them. Public librarians may well have to 'walk a fine line between a commercial and a public world' (Greenhalgh et al.1995), but as professionals they should know when to stay on the side of the public. However, as the experience of one respondent indicates, the:

> Culture has changed drastically from an old style 'benevolent' authority to a more business oriented organization. There has been an increased focus on customers but, at the same time, the more traditional public service values have come under threat and are now seen in a different perspective. The emphasis is on quality and value for money rather than ability, professional values and standards. (London borough)

As Govan (1988) has observed:

> This emphasis on economics over public service is attaining a certain vogue among librarians and receiving serious attention in our discussions and literature. Costs, of course have always been a basic concern but only as a means to providing services, sharing information, and stimulating learning.

In other words, public librarians must be committed to the public good and to the social purpose of their calling.

Sadly, however, 'libraries world wide are suffering spiritual deprivation as library managers strive to fit the mould carved by cost accountants. They are suffering narrowing of purpose and loss of direction as they concentrate more and more on their contribution to the economic bottom line (Cram 1995). The present survey suggests a number of reasons for this situation. In the first place, as one respondent wrote:

> The concept of the 'public service ethos' has been severely damaged by the government – and locally by its myopic supporters – since 1979. The constant attacks on local government through the removal of its powers, its influence and its scope for decision making has gone a long way to create local administration in place of local government. (English county)

The precise impact of this type of activity is, however, somewhat in doubt. As one respondent reported:

> A 'management of change' initiative was aimed at changing the culture of the whole county council organization. In many areas the change is rhetorical rather than actual. For example ** would claim that the 'public service ethos' has been increased. (English county)

Another librarian was of the opinion that 'public sector values and ethos are just starting to peek over the parapet again, as the market approach becomes a little tarnished' (English county). A further respondent spoke of 'some worrying trends and [argued that] public libraries need to consciously recognize that greater efficiency, cost effectiveness etc. must be tempered with the need to retain a public service ethos' (English county).

In some authorities the new ideas are being driven by senior management. One chief librarian told us:

> We have had two 'waves' of change with different chief executives. One (who didn't stay long) was very keen on 'commissioner/provider' models. The present one is much less enthusiastic for the 'commercial' approach. The hung nature of the council militates against a clean practical steer on such matters. (English county)

In another library:

> There's been a real 'anti-professional' culture across the council – the other side of 'customer first'. The feeling has been that professionals have dominated service provision, giving people what they thought they ought to have, and not taking account of customer views. This has meant a culture in which 'professional' is almost a dirty word. (London borough)

Others, too, need to be convinced of the value of professional or even paid librarians. For example, Katharine Whitehorn (1995), a journalist generally sympathetic to the library cause, recently suggested that public libraries should be partly staffed by volunteers. In a time of reduced opening hours and library closures she felt that volunteers should be used to keep public libraries open. Desperate times may call for desperate remedies, but such a course of action would mean that users would not receive the quality of service they deserve. In addition, it would threaten the livelihood of the many paraprofessionals currently employed in libraries. As has been indicated in Chapter 5, dealing with the public on a day-to-day basis requires staff to be properly trained and to have a proper knowledge of the stock and services. This can only be achieved if they are working on a full-time, or substantial part-time, basis. There may be a role for volunteers in helping to promote the library service, but it is unfair to expect them to be involved in the management and organization of its core activities.

This is an area where public librarians can legitimately learn from the experience of the private sector. The importance of employing suitably educated, skilled and trained frontline staff is demonstrated by the emphasis the best private services place on such activities. Airline check-in desks, hotel reception areas, bank counters and the like are not staffed by volunteers. Those responsible for such matters realize the value of employing people who are an integral part of their respective organizations. If, as a society, we feel that a job needs to be done, then we should be willing to pay for it. As a profession we need to persuade people with the skills of Ms. Whitehorn to help us communicate the case for adequate resources. The profession and the politicians responsible for funding must not be side-tracked by tempting but simplistic short-term solutions which, over the longer term, will seriously damage the quality of the services we offer.

Given the circumstances described above, it is not surprising that 'Professional librarians seem less sure of their role as more time is spent in managing' (English metropolitan district). Another librarian said that recent events had:

> . . . made me fundamentally review my professional and personal values. I reckon they are now in much sharper intellectual focus. I have also learned to adapt and be more clearly aware of when you have to compromise, and when principles are principles and not for trimming. (English county)

Professional principles are not entirely a thing of the past, but in the words of a number of respondents: 'The profession as a whole does not greatly influence the culture of the service' (English county), whereas 'Some fundamental issues and choices have had to be "faced up to" as a result of prevailing managerial culture' (London borough). In this new culture:

> The change from librarian to manager . . . marks the dropping of professionality in the higher reaches of the profession and acceptance of the meretricious values of unenlightened cost-accountancy (Roberts 1991).

Sadly, many of today's librarians, like others in public service, have been persuaded to take this unenlightened route. They have been told to reject the ideas, and indeed the values, of the past and some former young Turks of the profession now look to commerce rather than community for their inspiration.

It is interesting to reflect on how this revolution has been brought about. Part of the answer, we suggest, lies with the deliberate use – or rather misuse – of language. A character in Martin Amis' *The information* observes that 'in the business of reinvention, the first act is that of renaming' (Amis 1995). In the beginning is the word. The New Right were quick to recognize that 'it is necessary to make changes at the level of language before changing organizational processes and practices. Britain has been important internationally in providing the new market language' (Walsh 1995). Unfortunately, it has been taken up with enthusiasm by some public librarians, as anyone who has recently attended a professional conference will know, and Figure 10.3 demonstrates. This shows that no less than 84% of respondents to the present study believed that the use of private sector language had increased or greatly increased over the past five years.

One manifestation of this is the word now most commonly used to describe the people who use our public library services. The joint Sheffield/Loughborough project on TQM revealed that almost 50% of authorities now use the word 'customer', with the remainder using a variation on the theme of borrower, reader or user.

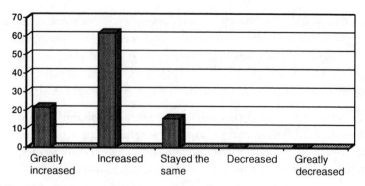

Fig. 10.3   *Use of private sector language*

This is more than a trivial issue, for in a very real sense what we call the people who use our services defines how we serve them. Professor David Marquand recently explained how 'the Thatcher and Major governments have redefined the citizen as customer, society as supermarket and the state as a kind of Securicor. Those who can, shop; those who can't, beg. Inside the supermarket anything goes. On the streets huddle the excluded' (Marquand 1993).

Such a redefinition of language, and the acceptance of the world it represents, makes it that much more difficult to empower people so that every citizen is able equally to take part in the decision-making process, whether that be in the workplace, the local community or the state. 'Becoming a customer (even if your rights are spelled out in a glossy charter) reduces political power (however limited), replacing it with a rule-based quasi contractual complaints system' (Cochrane 1993).

The fundamental consumerist message of the Citizen's Charter is demonstrated by the place of the apostrophe. It is an imperfect conception of citizenship that sees it in terms of individual rights rather than membership of a community. By accident or design, the Citizen's Charter reduces the power of the citizen. Michael Ignatieff (1988) recently explained how:

> . . . as a citizen I have become poorer . . . I can't use my tax cut money to repair the pavement outside my door . . . I cannot get my street lights repaired . . . I cannot spend the money on improving my son's decrepit school.

For public libraries the time has come to do away with what David Edgar (1991) has called the 'C word'. However, such has been the debasement of our professional language over the past decade that it is now widely accepted by people who should really know better. There are, though, some interesting divisions of opinion. One council 'will not use the term customer, [because] it smacks too much of buying a pound of sugar over the counter' (elected member). However, in another it was claimed that the customer concept had enabled them to 'move the service forward on a business footing; prior to the use of the word customer, things were much too wishy washy'. One might be forgiven for thinking that this is part of the management-speak rhetoric that has caused some users, such as those responding to the DNH survey, to have such a false perception of the present and future state of the service. To quote Gerald Kaufmann (1995), 'if you think services will magically improve because you use the word customer you are living in Cloud Cuckoo Land'.

Hoadley (1995) recently explained her unease at the term, stating:

> For some time the word customer has gnawed at me, somehow not feeling right. When I checked a dictionary, I knew why I was bothered by the term. A customer, by definition, is someone who 'purchases a commodity or service'. On the other hand, a user is someone who carries out a purpose or action availing oneself of something as a means or instrument to an end.

Another word that has been used to persuade librarians and other public sector workers to reject their professional values is 'elitism'. As illustrated in the previous chapter, some on the Left have apparently been taken in by the arguments that are used by the likes of Rupert Murdoch and other icons of the enterprise society. In journals of the Right, for instance, the word elitism is used to criticize the idea of the welfare state. Hence, in *Business week*, a publication whose readers complain that 'real capitalism hasn't happened yet'. (Morgan 1996), there are attacks on 'elitist education system[s] . . . that stress . . . state intervention and the role of civil servants in running government' (Javerski 1996). The same issue of the magazine goes on to warn middle America against 'intellectuals [another popular target of the populist Right] who believe that European social welfare policies should be a blueprint for action' (Becker 1996).

The DNH review suggested that public libraries are, at the moment, reasonably well managed, although there is some dissatisfaction, particularly among younger staff, because of the constraints under which they work. However, public libraries are facing a recruitment and leadership time bomb. Apart from a committed few, the best graduates from our best library schools no longer see public librarianship as a preferred career. Some more senior members of the profession have become so demoralized that they no longer have the courage of their convictions, or indeed even know what their convictions are. A leading academic librarian wrote recently:

> I meet public librarians regularly . . . And I fear for them. The great driving force of public libraries for a long period of time was the Carnegie spirit of learning and self improvement. For a large number of perfectly honourable and selfless reasons, public libraries seem to an outsider to have lost their way (Law 1996).

One might wonder in passing whether public librarians would be in such a position if they had received a similar kind of financial injection as that provided to the academic sector by the Follet Committee, but the substantial point remains. It is one that is recognized by insiders as well as outsiders. One chief librarian has asked, 'Is there a public library movement in 1990s Britain, and, if so, who are its leaders?' (Owen 1995). In the context of the present argument we might also ask what, if anything, distinguishes a leader from a manager? According to one writer:

> The distinction . . . can be summarized by the word purpose. Leaders create energy by instilling purpose. Managers control and direct energy. Leaders define success in terms of the accomplishment of a business achievement, the success of a product or service. Managers define success according to measures that are derived from the process of business independent of the content of the business. Leaders appeal to the higher values, the long-term potential of the individual to feel part of, a contributor to, achievements of mankind. The manager appeals to the immediate needs for income, status, and security. Leadership brings out the creativity of the individual and inspires courage. Management without leadership produces conformity. (Miller, quoted by Glenn nd).

Many of the submissions to the public library review expressed concern at the quality of leadership in the public library service. To help overcome these problems, the review team suggested a number of initiatives to help attract high-calibre recruits and provide professional leaders for the future. These included new DFEE (Department for Education and Employment) studentships, supernumerary trainee schemes, and a staff college to develop future professionals. All these ideas have considerable merit but, as the next chapter suggests, more needs to be done if public librarians are to confront the larger issues and 'rise above the mediocrity introduced by the disease of managementitis'.

Chapter 11

What can we do?

THE PROBLEMS IDENTIFIED in earlier chapters require positive action from practitioners and those library educators and policy makers with an interest in public libraries. There has been a positive response from the British Library to that part of the public library review that dealt with recruitment and leadership, but it can only provide a little of what is required. The public library profession will need to heal itself with respect to many of the issues discussed above.

It is said with some – although not total justification – that the library and information studies (LIS) schools are now the major recruitment agencies for the profession, although it should be noted that most of the students accepted for postgraduate librarianship programmes have been preselected for the profession by practising librarians. Be that as it may, the librarianship and information studies departments in the universities do have a real responsibility in terms of professional selection. It is one that should be taken seriously, and it is a little surprising to hear that some home students are offered places at library schools without interview. With the exception of overseas candidates, where for obvious reasons one has to rely on sponsors' and referees' reports, Sheffield staff interview all the students who take the MA in Librarianship programme. This at least enables us to 'weed out' those who, although good on paper are, for various reasons, unsuitable for library and information work in practice.

Readers will appreciate that nowadays students are being prepared for a wide range of careers, and that LIS departments cannot make suitability for public libraries the only selection criterion. However, in all our candidates we look for evidence of good interpersonal skills, analytical ability and social and political awareness. We look above all for enthusiasm. Jimmy Porter's cry of anguish of a quarter of a century ago is just as relevant today:

> Oh heavens, how I long for a little ordinary human enthusiasm. Just enthusiasm – that's all. I want to hear a warm, thrilling voice cry out Hallelujah – Hallelujah! I'm alive (Osborne 1960).

We look, too, for intellectual ability – indeed, those students who wish to be awarded a DFEE library studentship will normally have to have obtained at least a 2:i degree. Although as a department we are pleased to accept good students who do not have a first or 2:i, there can be little doubt that such an arbitrary cut-off point means that we sometimes lose some suitable candidates. That said, it is difficult to agree with those who suggest that universities should totally disregard academic standards. There is some evidence that working-class students, and those from minority ethnic communities, are still underrepresented on library school programmes, as indeed they are in higher education in general. Given the current cutbacks in the university sector, little or no improvement is likely in the immediate future. However, a major reason for that problem is to be found much earlier in candidates' educational careers, in the social situations in which children's educational identities are constructed and assessed.

It is true that some of the American library schools did lower their academic requirements considerably, particularly for black students. However, colleagues with experience in the USA tend to suggest that that was affirmative action of the wrong kind, and that more often than not, it was not beneficial to either the student, the school or the library profession. There are very real problems in dealing with this issue, but it should not be beyond our powers to devise methods of assessment, involving perhaps both practitioners and teachers, that provide fairer ways of judging candidates from less advantaged backgrounds. The Library Association (1994b), noting that 'Anecdotal evidence suggests the LIS profession has remained largely invisible to cultural minorities in the United Kingdom', has issued a document setting out possible strategies to improve the recruitment, retention and development of 'cultural minority staff'.

In terms of recruitment to the public library sector in general, one has to add that, even if the library schools and library practitioners could agree on appropriate criteria, there would still be the question of funding. This problem could be circumvented to some extent if public library authorities would support students by means of paid traineeships or similar arrangements. A few years ago the author suggested a cooperative trainee scheme whereby a group of local authorities would join together to finance a number of studentships dedicated to those who wanted to pursue a public library career. A letter was sent to every chief librarian in the country. Many – indeed most – were supportive of the idea, but doubted whether they could 'sell' it to their politicians, particularly at a time of local government reorganization. Such a scheme would not cost a great deal of money. To match a DFEE library studentship and to pay the fees for a one-year postgraduate course would cost no more than £7000. To finance 20 such studentships across the country would cost each of the existing public library authorities less than £850 a year. Something of this kind is going to be required if public libraries are to be able to recruit the dynamic professionals they need to properly serve the users of the future, expand their role in society and seize the opportunities of the information age.

The profession needs to produce students and young professionals with a vision for the future of the service. These are unlikely to be supplied by the reductionist and mechanistic perspective of NVQs. The jury is still out on the value of the lower-level courses, but an NVQ should not be regarded as equal to a professional education programme. The pragmatic focus and fragmented nature of these courses leave little room for a critical discussion of values. One is aware why public librarians may be tempted to encourage their professional staff to take such a route, but if they do so they will be selling short not only their personnel, but also the people they seek to serve.

A number of years ago Julia Reid (1982), in her study of education and training for community information, found that:

> While there is considerable enthusiasm for a high level qualification in information and advice work, there is also apprehension at the prospect of the 'professionalization' of the service, especially among workers in community-based information and advice agencies. They fear that this would lead to elitism, inflexibility, patronizing and unsympathetic attitudes towards clients and an unwillingness to encourage feedback and discussion with the clients.

It is a view that may be shared by some public librarians. However, provided the initial selection procedures by library school and employer are stringent, such fears are largely groundless.

The apprehension among some public librarians may result from the way the library schools are perceived to have covered, or not covered, public libraries in their curriculum. We have written elsewhere (Usherwood & Vessey 1988) about the decline of public librarianship as a discipline, but more specifically in the field of management there is the general criticism that 'our generic curriculum, until very recently, neglected to develop in students a skill highly regarded in the public sector – the ability to interact with and manage diverse, external and mainly political interests' (Perry & Kraemer 1983).

Lichfield (quoted in Meikle 1996) argues that the skill of managing social equity needs to be taught alongside those of enterprise and efficiency. She states that managing in local government is 'harder than running a private business on well established market principles and requires a specialist body of knowledge'. Therefore, when teaching public library management, in addition to covering those management issues that are common to all organizations, it is necessary to include the management of the political process. Most of the people who attend LIS departments, certainly at postgraduate level, are of high academic quality, but more often than not one is disappointed by their level of political awareness. Although there are some notable exceptions, today's students are less aware of the practice and philosophy of politics than their counterparts of 20 years ago, and some are politically illiterate. It could be argued that creating political awareness is a job for secondary schools, but few seem to be undertaking the task.

At the start of the Sheffield MA programme students are introduced to the social and political context in general, and the politics of information in particular. This is especially important in terms of the present discussion, because the inequalities of the present time are largely an effect of the structure and forms of social organization. Librarians, like architects, social workers or anyone else involved in serving the public, need to be aware of this. The inequalities present in access to information and ideas are related to the primary inequalities inherent in the distribution of power, income and wealth. Such inequalities can provoke a variety of political responses, and students need to consider these via all the usual methods of seminars, lectures and essays.

It should, perhaps, be emphasized that the aim is not political indoctrination. The staff at Sheffield, as in other universities, exhibit a wide range of political views and it would be a naive teacher who believed that he or she could indoctrinate a group of very bright postgraduates. We do, however, want students to consider the political dimensions of their chosen career. We do want to increase their political awareness and raise questions in their minds.

In relating this to management it is necessary to emphasize the issues of public pressure and accountability, and the importance of understanding public behaviour, the difficulties of rationing, and of measuring or evaluating multidimensional activities. We should stress the benefits of managing for cooperation and interdependence rather than for competition. Stock management, as is emphasized in Chapter 9, must also be given adequate space in the curriculum. Above all, perhaps we need to create an understanding of the public library manager's responsibility to the wider society that exists outside his or her immediate organization.

Such issues can only be one part of a library school's curriculum. Overall, it is the job of library educators to develop in students a critical appreciation of current thought and practice in library and information work, to teach the basis skills employed in practice, and to introduce them to topics and ideas that will prepare them for future as well as immediate career opportunities. Subjects such as information retrieval, practical computing, resources and management are, of course, relevant to public librarians, but in our desire to incorporate the new librarianship and the new technology into our programmes we must not overlook those topics that are of proven and continuing value.

As in public libraries, in academia academic and social values are beginning to take second place to economic considerations. The tension of this situation was caught nicely by Malcolm Bradbury in his novel *Eating people is wrong'*. Some readers may recall the passage where the leading characters discuss the role of a university education:

> 'But why are we teaching in a university in the first place? Goodness knows it's not for the money . . . isn't it because we want to live in a world of circulating ideas and critical valuations? Isn't it because we love independence and freedom of thought? Or am I being naive?'
> 'In a way, Stuart, I really think you are', said Viola.
> 'Well, I don't', said Treece. 'If our function isn't to talk about what is good when the rest of the world is talking about what is profitable, what *can* we do?' (Bradbury 1978).

Now many academics talk about what is profitable on the reasonable basis that their students will go into business and industry. Many library students appear to want to take this road, and it has been predicted that by the year 2010 60% of the graduates of library schools will be self-employed or will work out of libraries under contract to small businesses. Practitioners and academics must work together if the public library service is to obtain a fair share of a severely reduced cake.

As a profession public librarians can sometimes appear surprisingly anti-intellectual, and antiprofessional as well. This is a dangerous and self-defeating stance. The public will be better served by a profession that recognizes the value and social significance of the skills its members possess. This is not an elitist view, however that is defined, but rather a recognition that there are groups of people who have special skills, skills that can be used to benefit society at large. Librarians are one such group.

As someone who has moved from practice to teaching to practice to teaching, the author believes it is wrong to exaggerate the gap between theory and practice, practitioners and library researchers. Moreover, we believe that some of the solutions to our present malaise will be found through a much more positive attitude to public library research. At the time of writing, the Society of Chief Librarians is considering areas for future research and we must await their conclusions, but we would argue that the following should appear high on their agenda:

- the public library and society;
- the public library and technology;
- the public library in the political arena;
- the public library and the economy;
- the public library and the new managerialism.

The need to measure the social impact of the public library has already been considered. A social audit of libraries was suggested in Chapter 6. In the present climate such an audit could provide information about the extent to which library authorities are attempting or withdrawing the provision of services for those who are not, or unlikely to be, library users. To coin a phrase, do we know if the public library service is going back to basics – and if it is, what those basics might be? An analysis along the lines described earlier could reveal the balance in the distribution of public library services. It could also raise fundamental questions regarding the equity of current services and the methods used to fund them. Social audit techniques could also be used to address many of the questions raised by Iain Sproat (1993) in his speech to the 1993 Public Library Authorities Conference. Take, for instance, the most contentious question of all, that regarding the public provision of reading. Using the techniques of social audit, perhaps linked with the uses and gratifications methodology of mass media researchers, we could learn more about the impact of reading on the individual and the community as a whole.

Also under the heading of the public library in society, it is important to consider the relationship, if any, between public libraries and the concept of citizenship. The Citizen's Charter has, as we have seen, had a major impact on public library management. The full impact of this, for good or ill, needs to be considered. Moreover, it is often presented as the Prime Minister's big idea for the country as a whole, and it behoves us to examine the role that public library services might play in providing information, identified several years ago as the fourth right of citizenship (National Consumer Council 1977). Do we know enough about the questions that come up in people's lives and the ways in which they go about obtaining answers? Do we know how this might change in the future? In addition, we need to learn more about the impact of social policy on the use and users of the public library service. For instance, what are the implications for public libraries, and the staff who work in them, of policies such as care in the community?

As argued elsewhere (Usherwood 1993b), that particular policy might require librarians to develop expertise in the therapeutic use of leisure. The public library could become a centre where people with disabilities could extend and use their artistic and other skills to the full. Here, as in other areas, the new communications technology may provide new forms of service: the public library could, for example, be a venue for computer painting and other activities that can help stimulate and develop the whole person. There is perhaps room for some 'blue sky' research to develop ideas of this kind.

As Chapter 3 indicates, there is a need for projects to look at the impact of IT on service delivery. How might it alter the way people use, or want to use, public libraries? Indeed, will there be a place for the public library when people are able to dial up a personalized electronic information, communications and entertainment menu? Will community information services be replaced by the technology of artificial intelligence? The comment of the Sheffield student mentioned in an earlier chapter ('a machine can't see somebody cry') raises interesting and significant questions about the importance of human interaction in a technological world. These are questions that we should be asking both as practitioners and as public library researchers. We need to question, too, how the available technology, and that which will soon be available, is affecting our decision-making processes in the management of library services. Is it, for instance, leading to greater centralization or decentralization?

A consideration of decision making leads quite naturally to the matter of politics and the politicians responsible for our services. Readers of this text will not need reminding that politics is important to the effective management of public libraries. It is therefore essential that we understand the way politicians think yet, as indicated in Chapter 2, the political dimension is rarely on the agenda when research topics are being discussed.

The Comedia report (*Borrowed time?* 1993) reminded us of the need for a fuller understanding of the economic impact of libraries, and there is little need to go over that ground again. However, it does seem that there are a number of other economic areas that we might address. In the first place we should examine public libraries as economic institutions in their own right. For instance, little research appears to have been carried out into the contribution made by public libraries to the wellbeing of the private sector. There have been a number of projects illustrating their economic contribution through services to industry and commerce, but very little has been said about library expenditure in the private sector, or about the degree to which different parts of the private sector depend on well-funded public services, or the extent to which employment in some private sector companies is related to public library expenditure. As part of this debate we might also investigate how far the presence of a public library encourages, or for that matter discourages, people to use a shopping centre or, more specifically, to purchase books and the other items on display in public libraries.

It is has been argued in this text and elsewhere that the culture of public service in the UK has undergone dramatic change in recent years. These changes have been brought about as the result of financial constraints, information technology, the ideology of the Thatcher and Major governments, and the importation of management techniques developed largely in the commercial sector. As researchers we need to ask questions about the appropriateness or otherwise of the new managerialism to public library services. It was to this end that Margaret Evans and the author undertook the joint project described in Chapter 4 and, in part, why this book was written. There are many other topics associated with the new managerialism that require further investigation, and from a different viewpoint to that of the present author. These might range from an analysis of mission statements, 'customer care' and performance-related pay, to a study of its impact on the equity of service delivery, and indeed the present culture of public library organizations.

One of the best definitions of organizational culture is that used by Schein (1985). He states that:

> Organizational culture is the pattern of basic assumptions that a given group has invented, discovered or developed, in learning to cope with its problems of external adaptation and internal integration, and that has worked well enough to be considered valid, and therefore to be taught to new members as the correct way to perceive, think, and feel . . . It is not . . . the philosophy or value system which the founder may articulate or write down in various 'charters'. Rather, it is the assumptions which lie behind the values and which determine the behaviour patterns and the visible artefacts such as architecture, office layout, dress codes and so on.

It is the job of researchers to test some of those assumptions.

Wagner (1992), in her interesting book *Public libraries as agents of communications: a semiotic analysis*, has gone some way towards this in an Australian context. Although it is not a text that can be recommended as an easy read, it does provide an interesting theoretical underpinning to some important practical issues. It also raises some important questions. What does librarianship mean to the state? What does it mean to the librarian? Why are there different perceptions of public purpose, not just between the local authority and the profession, but between different professionals, and between professionals and users? Such questions are as valid here as they are in Australia. They also serve to remind us that we have yet to develop an underpinning philosophy for public librarianship.

One is, of course, aware that, in the words of *The British Library research bulletin*, public librarians are 'very much bound up in day-to-day practical problems, requiring pragmatic, or political solutions in short order'. However, it is important that we do not spend so much time on the short term and the obvious that we fail to grasp the opportunity to develop a philosophy that will be significant in the long term, for both the public library profession and the people it seeks to serve.

The profession is badly placed to investigate practical problems and/or political solutions 'in short order'. We need urgently to devise a mechanism whereby topical issues can be thoroughly investigated in a timely way. The British Library is to be congratulated on the quick way in which it responded to the request for funding an investigation into the impact of the Sheffield library strike (Proctor et al. in press), but there are, and always will be, other important issues where the ability to react quickly to circumstances would improve the information available to professionals and decision makers. For example, professionals and politicians need to know the impact on users of service point closure. Latest statistics

(Loughborough University 1994) reveal that between 1988/9 and 1993/4 the total number of public library service points fell by 183 (3.6%), including mobile library service points. During the same period the number of service points open more than 45 hours per week fell by over 17%. These 'broad-brush' figures hide huge variations in performance. Sheffield Libraries, for example, lost over 34% of its opening hours during the same five-year period. 1995 saw further reductions in public library budgets, and evidence from professionals in the field suggests that there may be other authorities proposing closures in 1996/7. The figures also hide the number of building-based service points that may have been replaced by mobile library stops.

Here is an issue of some importance, but it is one of the least-researched fields in public library management and service delivery. Neither The Library Association nor the Library Campaign maintains a record of public library service point closures, and neither is able to provide a definitive list of either service points or library authorities that have been subject to closure or significant interruption of service during the last ten years. A preliminary search of the literature reveals no published research on the impact on users of either service point closure or reductions in opening hours. In addition, little internal research has surfaced.

At the time of writing staff at the University of Sheffield are awaiting the results of a research application to examine:

- the impact of public library service point closure on the library user;
- the impact of opening hours reductions on the library user;
- the relative impact of closure vs. opening hours reductions on the use of services.

The proposal has been before potential funders for several months and nobody is really to blame for the delay, but this is just the kind of work that would benefit from a dedicated fund for research into topical issues in which time is of the essence.

Over the years there have been many excellent research projects, but generally their impact outside the profession has been limited. In this respect we can learn from the Comedia experience. That report's admirable suggestions for research into the public library's economic and social impact, its strategic buying power and the need for sophisticated performance indicators had all been adequately covered in the professional literature well before Comedia saw the light of day, yet they had received relatively little notice. It is perhaps indicative of public library researchers' lack of clout and marketing nous that it took a group of outside consultants to bring such ideas to public and professional attention.

If researchers from within the profession are to obtain a higher profile there must be much more cooperation between those involved. We have already mentioned one project that is the result of cooperation between Loughborough and

Sheffield Universities, and despite the obvious difficulties there is room for further such cooperative projects involving those few library school academics who still maintain an interest in public libraries. Such cooperation should also involve colleagues from the European schools, to help us develop a European perspective to our research and to help us in our search for a philosophical basis.

Likewise, we require more joint proposals involving LIS Departments and practitioners. In addition, as the DNH review demonstrated, a combination of all the talents involving practitioners, private sector researchers and the universities can provide a very potent forum for public library research, and one that will enable us to compete on equal terms with the large consultancies from well outside our professional field, who are nevertheless taking an increasing interest in the public library sector.

Of course, there must always be the opportunity for the individual researcher and there will be times when the workings of the Higher Education Funding Council and research assessment exercises will lead to rivalry rather than cooperation between university departments. However, that having been said, we must work together to develop a research agenda that will take the public library service into the 21st century. We must be in a position to 'undertake the fundamental research and reappraisal that is so essential to our survival' (Owen 1985).

For research to have an impact the results must be made known. There is an urgent need to establish a centre for the effective dissemination of public library research, to make known not just the work that is carried out in academic institutions, but also the 'hidden research' that is carried out as part of the day-to-day management of public libraries. Funding will be needed to establish such a research and consultancy unit, but it would be money very well spent indeed. In addition, there is a need for a research presence within public libraries, and library managers should seriously consider adding research officers to their establishment. The difficulties of getting approval for such posts as specialisms of all kind are being cut back are not to be underestimated. However, it should be an integral part of public library management to monitor research output, identify in-house research opportunities and liaise with the research community in library schools and other organizations.

Public library researchers, in common with those in other disciplines, undertake a number of functions. They seek to clarify the issues to be researched and select appropriate methodologies to undertake the task. They then use those methodologies to obtain data and finally to analyse and interpret the evidence they have collected. At this final stage, if they are honest they also admit to any limitations in their research. It is a process from which the whole profession can benefit and to which many, not just academics, can contribute. The future of the public library service will, to a significant extent, depend on the quality of its research base.

It will also depend on the operation of the recently established Library and Information Commission. It is too early to make a judgment on the impact of this body. Like the LIS departments discussed earlier, it is not only concerned with public libraries but it is potentially a significant power in the land. It is therefore vital that public librarians ensure that the public library service is placed high on the Commission's agenda. Some comfort may be gained from the fact that the chairperson of the Commission (Evans 1996b) has expressed a special interest in public libraries, and regards it as the job of the Commission to raise their status with senior politicians, civil servants and other decision makers. He believes this can be achieved via a Saatchi and Saatchi advertising campaign and by the profession, and the Library Association in particular, being less confrontational with the present (at the time of writing Conservative) government. It is a point of view and a technique that has apparently worked for him in the past, but it is difficult to see what else the library profession could have done when faced with an administration that deliberately set out to confront the principles and practice of the public service professions.

Chapter 12

Rediscovering public library management

A S THIS TEXT has shown, the past few years have seen significant change for those who work in the public library service. The immediate past has not been good for libraries or the people they serve. In the 1980s the shopping mall replaced the town hall and public library as a symbol of the age, and although the dark diva of the enterprise culture is now safely consigned to the slag heap of history, we are still living with the consequences of the many crimes committed in her name. Perhaps the greatest of these was to take away hope and idealism from a whole generation, perhaps two. Too many believed in 'Tina' ('There is no alternative').

Something similar happened in the library world. A short time ago the author was taken to task by an apparently distraught librarian who thought it 'outdated drivel' that we should continue to promote the value of libraries (Cheese 1994). Most library educators will know of students who have had doubts about their choice of career because they have heard somewhere that the public library and public service are things of the past.

In a recent book (St Clair 1994b) we were told that our 'connections with education and social work have effectively diminished the role of the information provider . . . to that of a subservient delivery agent'. At the same time, on professional platforms sharp-suited librarians contemptuously dismiss their users as 'punters', and 'customer' seems to be the preferred term in over 50% of our public libraries (Evans et al. in press). We have travelled a long way, albeit in the wrong direction, since we discussed the fourth right of citizenship.

After the dreary decade that was the 1980s, when greed and apathy ruled in equal parts, it is time for public librarians to retrieve a sense of idealism and revisit the social and political issues that help or hinder the information professions and the people that use them. It is this centrality of social over financial values that makes the management of public library services different, and so complicates the measurement of their performance.

There are alternatives to greed and apathy, and still sources of hope. For instance, Will Hutton (1996a), in his excellent review of the state of our nation, has observed that the idea of the welfare state is deeply ingrained in the British psyche, while, more specifically in our own field, the DNH public library review has shown that the British place a high value on the public library. Many library staff still maintain a sense of service and community despite appalling odds. As we write there is beginning to be a smell of death about the 'greed is good' philosophy, and signs that we may yet return to a more civilized and compassionate way of life. The past few years should cause us to look back in anger, but the history of the public library movement gives us some reason to look forward with hope.

The DNH public library review revealed the tension in the public library service between stability and change. The public are satisfied with the services they receive, but the 'reformers' of the New Right feel the need to destroy the structure that has successfully delivered this service. At the same time, the professionals are at odds with the public's evaluation. They know that much more could be achieved with better resources and feel that public expectations are too low. The review also suggested that there is a danger that new ideas and opportunities might be too easily overlooked because of the parameters set by our past experience.

The challenge for today's public librarians is to consider management in terms of the distinctive function and values of the public service ideal, but in such a way that will allow the service to remain an effective social force in the next century and beyond. We must renew the distinctive purpose of the public library as a cultural institution. In so doing we must challenge the inappropriate use of private sector techniques and the over-reliance on the market. The professional librarian who becomes a manager will inevitably experience a degree of tension. However, if the poacher is to become a gamekeeper, he or she must keep the heart of the poacher. The techniques of management must be the servant of a community-based public library service, and not its master. The profession must rediscover the public library culture, with its concern for professional ethics and individual and community needs.

If we allow our public service and cultural institutions to be handed over to managerialists whose only concern is to make a profit, they will quickly be levelled down to the lowest common denominator. The press and electronic media already provide numerous examples of this depressing transition. In making this point, we should not be too worried about accusations of paternalism or elitism. Some forms of paternalistic practice are easy – almost too easy – targets, but it should not be forgotten that many of the early public libraries came about as the result of the work of philanthropists and reformers. Moreover, if one has to make a choice between the public service paternalism of the BBC, public libraries and other civic institutions, or the products of the media moguls and the free market, then paternalism does not seem such a bad option.

For all its faults, the public service ethic has provided people with many opportunities to grow and develop. Dennis Potter's comments on the BBC are relevant here. In recalling the BBC he joined, he said:

> I'm not saying that world wasn't paternalistic, and I am not saying that it can be preserved as it was, and I am not saying that there mustn't be change, but that world was based on a sense of assumptions that are almost now derisible, laughable . . . I was given the space to grow into, and I gave, I gave my working life to it as a result . . . Whereas if I was starting now, where would I get that chance? (Potter 1994).

We might ask similar questions of public librarians. Should the profession, for example, have a set of assumptions about what is good and bad literature? Is it more paternalistic to follow the tabloid route and consider our users as dimwits, or to provide them with opportunities to develop ?

Public servants have also become a little too afraid of the idea of bureaucracy. One respondent to the present study, admittedly in the minority, said:

> One of the worst features of old style local government was the 'can't be done' culture. Even with considerably less resources than ever before, I still feel positive that we *can* do exciting things. (London borough, original emphasis)

However, as Murray and Letch (1987) remind us, 'bureaucracy is such a dirty word that it is easy to forget its benefits'. Although it is true that bureaucracy can some times slow progress in the way suggested by the respondent quoted above, we should not overlook what has been done by the public service-oriented librarians of the past. In addition, bureaucracy is a way of ensuring the impartial and equitable expression of collective decisions.

Elected members, as a part of the local government bureaucracy, are much maligned but they 'are accountable representatives [who have] to hold the line for the common good and for public values such as fairness, equality, environment and the local economy, and for the long term future' (Gaster 1995). There is a danger that this benign bureaucracy will be replaced by a managerialist market-led bureaucracy that neither cares about nor understands the concept of public service. Those of us concerned with public service must be aware of the adverse effects on local, and for that matter national, democracy of some of the managerialist ideas discussed in this book.

The public library manager must seek to accentuate the positive aspects of bureaucracy while eliminating its constraining ones. Public librarians do not have to reject public service values in favour of private sector management techniques. They will, however, have to be flexible enough to learn how to deliver public services better. To do this they will need to be free from the feeling of fear identified in the opening chapter. As Mark Tully (1993) has pointed out, 'Fear is far more constricting than . . . bureaucracy. In a large organization it puts a high premium on sycophancy and virtually rules out healthy criticism of the management.' We must, then, have respect for our staff and their motivation. As Flynn (1993) observes, 'If they do not get satisfaction from their work they will not generate satisfaction in service users'.

The public library service must be managed in line with a distinctive public service ethic. The public librarian needs to be responsive to the needs of his or her community, and to have a set of core values. He or she must be flexible enough to deal with a changing world, but strong enough to resist the fads of fashion and the siren voices of populist management gurus, who neither know nor care for the public library service. It is for the future leaders of the public library profession to understand the nature of the changing circumstances and to formulate an appropriate professional response and develop a vision for the future. They must communicate that vision to their colleagues in local government, to users and potential users, to politicians and other stakeholders. In developing a vision managers must listen to the people who work in our libraries and seek to encourage them, so as to ensure a consistency between the professional vision of the service and what happens in practice.

The public library professional is one of a number of people with a stake in the service, and all stakeholders need to be taken into account when considering what is meant by the quality of the service. In this sense public library management is a collective undertaking. Of course we must consult and listen to our users and potential users, and seek to empower them in a way that is more meaningful than that derived from the limited power to purchase or not to purchase.

However, public library management cannot be based on the doctrine of individualism: the various interests have to be balanced as well as met. Public library management must incorporate a range of interests: those of the user and the citizen, the voter and the worker, the professional and the politician. The good public librarian will be sensitive to the fact that elected members have a political agenda. 'In the best of councils that will increasingly mean an understanding that enables the manager to debate and challenge that agenda, testing its capacity for effective implementation' (Kerley 1994). Public library managers must be prepared to debate politics as well as management.

We must measure and evaluate our performance in a way that communicates with users and demonstrates success, and leads to the better use of resources in the attainment of social objectives. The funding of the service should reflect not just the volume of use but also the social benefits achieved. Mrs Thatcher, when she gave her patronizing lectures on economics, used to make a great play of the way ordinary people managed their budgets, but somehow these images were never translated into local government. We know from personal experience that when we make a purchase few of us decide to buy or not on the basis of price alone. We make some judgment on the trade-offs between price and quality, reliability, the ethics of the organization and so forth. In public services the same judgments need to be made. Too often, simple cost cutting results in a poorer service rather than any genuine increase in productivity.

Resources are a major problem, and quite clearly more are required by the public library service. There now seems to be a conventional wisdom that Britain can no longer afford its public services. Mantras about 'not throwing money at a problem' and/or low taxes are repeated ad nauseam by politicians. In a way they represent the most dangerous legacy of Thatcherism. They are the product of a society based on personal gain. They are also nonsense, and dangerous nonsense at that. The social consequences of a more unequal society will not be pleasant. Somehow we must rid ourselves of the 'selfish gene' and recognize that we depend on each other. We must be prepared to make our contribution to the common weal. This means that many of us (the author included) should pay a higher standard rate of tax. If politicians are so afraid of the tabloid trash that they will not express that fact, then the professions must. The medical profession has done just that.

Public librarians, then, must be prepared to express their belief in the public library as an institution. This is a belief that can be fully justified by its past, not to mention the findings of numerous research projects. To be proud of the public library, to be proud of the profession, is not an expression of elitism or professional arrogance. Such professional pride in what we do would mark a return to the self-confidence that has been dissipated by the events of recent years. It will not be easy: the destruction wrought to libraries and other cultural, civilizing and caring institutions has been so great that it may take a generation to rebuild, not just their fabric but the confidence of those they employ. Public service convictions must resurface, and considerations beyond those of the bottom line prevail. In short, we must rediscover *public* library management.

Appendix 1

The DNH public library review –
a researcher's perspective

IT WAS JUST before Christmas 1993 when I received a telephone call inviting me to become a member of team that was to submit a research proposal to the Department of National Heritage (DNH) which was looking for consultants to carry out a review of the public library service in England and Wales. Thus started one of the most intense, stimulating and frustrating periods of my professional life. I have introduced that personal note because, like a nervous civil servant, I should make it clear that this section reflects my personal view of the process involved.

The brief for the project called for an examination of:

- The changing world within which public libraries have to operate. This required that the consultants take account of economic and political parameters, social, demographic and technological change, and changes in local government.
- The services commonly provided as part of a modern public library service and expected by the public. This was to include services not necessarily required under the 1964 Act that governs public libraries in England and Wales. The work had also to include a review of recent significant developments.
- The changing and emerging needs of the public, taking into account the results of public consultation.
- Partnerships and links with other library sectors and with related sectors, including the voluntary and private sectors.
- Relationships between library services and other local authority services.

'The review', said the then minister Peter Brooke (1994), would:

. . . provide a fundamental restatement of purpose for the public library service and is one of the Department's most important initiatives. It is designed to ensure that libraries remain as vital an inspiration to future generations in the next century as they have been in this.

Our team, under the banner of the Aslib Consultancy, made a presentation to a tender selection board that considered submissions from a number of organizations, including some private sector companies from outside the library and information world. Readers would need to ask officials at the Department of National Heritage as to why our group was chosen in preference to the others that applied. Rumour has it that it was described by a member of the board as a team of all the talents. It is not of course proper for the author to comment on that but it was certainly a team of all the attitudes. It included at the outset private sector consultants and a broad range of academic opinion. Two senior practising librarians also became an integral part of the group once the contract had been awarded.

Before the final report (Aslib 1995) was published *The Observer* newspaper referred to 'a bitter behind-the-scenes battle between the advocates of the well-funded free public library service and the proponents of market forces' (Hughill 1995). This is not an accurate description of the Aslib deliberations, but it is true that such battles were and are being fought in some parts of the public library community. It is, however, to the credit of the Project Director, John Myers, that although the research team engaged in vigorous debate, the discussions were never bitter.

Some members of the team had to revisit and re-evaluate some cherished professional philosophies, whereas others had to be persuaded that such philosophies were important, or even existed. This range of opinion and background meant that we were nothing if not even-handed in our approach to the task. Moreover, we worked with a steering committee that included leading practitioners and politicians, who provided us with additional guidance and viewpoints. The variety of attitudes and experience present in the team was revealed in some very interesting and stimulating discussions, some of them of a transatlantic variety. These sometimes reflected different views about the way that we should interpret the data, or indeed what data were valid – an issue that has also been discussed throughout this text.

The DNH public library review in fact included six substantial research projects, timetabled to be carried out in a period of just 12 months. In the end we had a database of evidence containing over a million words, but the time constraints meant that there was little time for scholarly reflection on the mass of data obtained. This was a source of frustration for an academic researcher, but it does mean that there is much in the files that will be of interest to future workers in the field. The projects undertaken by the team involved:

- in-depth interviews with 922 people in their homes;
- a postal survey sent to 3600 people whose names appeared on the electoral role in nine case study areas;
- a detailed set of questions sent to 3400 staff currently working in public libraries;

- eighteen group discussions with 144 library staff in nine case study areas;
- in-depth interviews with political leaders and chief executives.

Much of the research was undertaken in nine case study areas. These were chosen to reflect the different types of authority and geographical region, but we also carried out a sixth piece of research, namely an omnibus survey to check the representativeness of the other surveys. One of the authorities surveyed is in Wales, and we therefore had to translate our research instruments to accommodate the needs of Welsh speakers.

The project also included a review of the current, past and historic literature in the field and the analysis of evidence invited from a variety of organizations. In addition, the research team received approximately 3000 comments as a result of a poster campaign and a leaflet distributed by The Library Association. Some of these comments have been included in the main body of this book.

There was also an extensive consultation exercise following the publication of the draft report, and members of the team addressed a large number of meetings with professionals, politicians and members of the public. Most fair-minded observers would agree that the research team took on board many of the comments that came their way as part of this consultation exercise, and this fact is reflected in the final report.

Altogether, the DNH review represents the most intensive survey of public library users, non-users and staff carried out anywhere in the world. Our approach meant that we gathered, cross-checked and combined data from a variety of perspectives. This process of triangulation helped to avoid problems of bias and improve the validity of the findings. The data quoted in the report have a high level of reliability, with at least a 95% statistical significance and in many instances better than 99%.

As indicated earlier, the surveys of users and non-users were an integral and essential part of the project. When the Aslib team made its original presentation to the DNH's selection board it gave four major reasons for finding out the views of users. These were:

- to see whether the public's perception of the public library had changed or not;
- to help the provision of appropriate services;
- to evaluate the public library's place in the community;
- to evaluate the case for public funding.

To help consider these issues it was felt necessary to obtain information on the following:

- How much use is made of the public library? In looking at this the team was aware that statistics do not tell the whole story, and that the value of libraries

should be judged on more than just membership and issue figures.
- Who are the users and non-users of the public library? There was and is a great deal of research in this area, and this is reflected in the final report. However, much of the previous work tends to tell us who the users are, but rather less about why they use libraries. Thus it was also necessary to find out what uses are made of the public library? and What uses *could* be made of the public library? This was important for a project that looked to the future. Such questions also provide information on the extent of both public and professional horizons.
- How people use the public library?
- How people would like to use the public library in the future? Again, this was a question that looked forward and asked people to consider how methods of use might change, perhaps as a result of technological developments.
- What do people use library materials and information for?: There is a need to find out much more about the impact of library material, especially perhaps that of imaginative literature, on the individual. Our data revealed some answers, but there is still scope for much more research in this area.
- Are people satisfied when they use the library?: At the original presentation to the tender selection board I expressed the opinion that people are 'pathetically grateful' for the library services they receive, and my view is the same today.
- Are people aware of the services available?: It was clear to the team that to just ask people what services they use would be very limiting, as they might not be aware of what is available, or what could be made available in the future. Any analysis of the data must take account of this, and it is a point we shall return to later.

The need to understand the requirements of users has long been recognized as being an important prerequisite for the effective delivery of public library services. Furthermore, as the Hillingdon Project (Totterdell & Bird 1976) demonstrated, all those years ago, attitudes to services can be an important help or hindrance to the effective library. Equally, it has been shown that survey research is a powerful tool to help understand user requirements. Surveys allow direct communication from users and potential users without their views being filtered through other interests. The data obtained can then be employed to ensure that library services are more closely aligned to the needs of the different communities being served.

A principle adopted in the user survey was that 'the individual is the primary authority on his [or her] own actions and experience' (Brown & Sime 1981). We were very keen to obtain a qualitative response, being aware that the value and significance of public library use cannot be ascertained by figures alone. Statistics can only provide part of the picture, as Chapter 6 of this book demonstrates. The in-depth home interviews were a vital source of qualitative data, as indeed were the many submissions we received from individuals and organizations.

In particular we received many submissions from senior citizens, emphasizing the importance of the library service in their lives. Their comments testify that figures alone cannot do justice to the value of the public library to this section of the community or, for that matter, any other. This is not a line of thought that always appeals to quantitative researchers, or indeed to the advocates of the new managerialism, but often the beneficial impact of the library experience was most graphically described in the letters and comments we received. Some of these are reproduced in the final report and in this book, but they are only the tip of a considerable iceberg and it is to be hoped that further analysis of both the statistical data bank and the text database will be undertaken in the future.

As is the case with any survey that involves the general population, it was important to use the simplest possible words to convey our exact meaning. For similar reasons our approach to respondents was kept as informal as possible. In preparing the research instruments we were also very conscious of the need not to ask leading and presuming questions. This is of course good research technique, but we were also aware of the rumours about hidden agendas that were circulating within the library profession, a product, one suspects, of the distrust felt for the present government by many of those who work in public services.

In the survey questions and the interview schedules great care was taken not to lead respondents. For example, when asking questions dealing with sensitive or controversial areas respondents were given a choice. Thus a question asking about the controversial area of funding read as follows:

Q15: Suppose your public library needs extra resources to keep up services, to which one course of action would you give top priority?
Tick one box only

Raise council tax so that more can be spent on libraries	[]
Raise income tax or VAT to allow for increased central government grants to public libraries	[]
Charge library users for all services, including borrowing books	[]
People in the county or borough to vote to set up a new fund just for public libraries paid into by all local households	[]
Cut back services, with fewer books and shorter opening hours	[]
Rely on volunteers and sponsors to fill the gap	[]
Close your library	[]
Don't know, or decline to say	[]

This particular question also provides a mini case study on the interpretation of data. In giving respondents such a wide range of options we made life a little difficult for ourselves. At first glance the barchart summarizing the results presented in the report would seem to suggest that people favour charging. However, this is in some ways misleading, because if all those respondents who support public funding options are added together they clearly outweigh those who want to impose charges. We should perhaps have included a chart showing this. If we had, it would have looked like Figure A1.1.

As the report makes clear, further analysis revealed that those people who support charging are tentative in their opinions and include a high proportion of occasional and non-users. As readers will know, in the light of these findings the review recommends that 'the principle of free and equal access to library materials should be extended when conditions allow' and makes 'a case for allowing uncharged access to those Internet or World Wide Web sources that are essentially "free". '

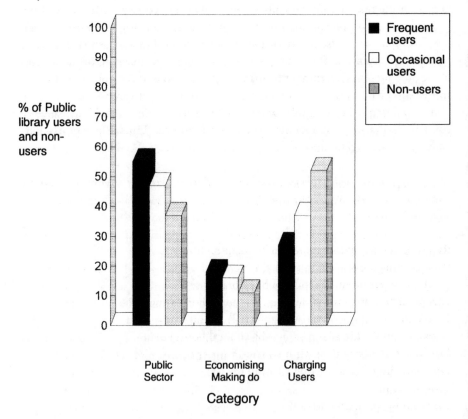

Fig. A1.1 *Opinions on funding of public libraries – choice of options*

A major strength of the DNH review is that it brought together public, political and professional opinions. In principle an assessment of the public library service can be made by all of these groups, but it would be too simplistic to suggest that all groups are equally able to make such judgments about all aspects of the service. This point, and other issues involved in the evaluation of public services, are discussed throughout the present text.

Overall, the DNH survey has shown that public libraries have a generally favourable image with all groups. The public library is, in short, a very popular institution. This may lend some weight to the view expressed at the outset that users and potential users are too easily satisfied. It may also be the reason behind one of the more surprising and disturbing factors arising from the DNH study, that is the differences between public and professional perceptions of the state of the public library service. The data show that only a relatively small number of users feel that the public library service is deteriorating; indeed, on balance they feel that it has improved in the last five years and that it is likely to improve. This is in strict contrast to the views expressed by professional librarians. The dangers of taking management, or indeed political, decisions on the basis of users' perceptions alone are obvious, especially when, as is argued in the main text, the new managerialists tell us to get close to the customer. Simplistically applied, such an idea would lead to a significant decline in the quality of our public library service.

For this and other reasons the Aslib review team also considered it important to examine the attitudes and perceptions of library staff. Hence staff in the nine case study areas were also asked to respond to some of the questions that were put to users and non-users. Moreover, given the changing circumstances in the library and information world, it was essential to ascertain staff attitudes to innovation and change. Work on this aspect of the study was largely carried out by two members of the team, who used a 'tool kit' in the case study authorities to measure 'the readiness of individuals, groups and organizations to react positively to innovations and promote change'.

The 'organizational health check' used in the research had previously been used successfully with a public library and other public sector organizations (Wallis 1993). This instrument asked staff to comment, by means of a Likert scale, on the culture of their organization, staffing matters such as managers' competence, selection and recruitment, internal communications, organizational structures, knowledge of users, financial management and relations with library suppliers. Staff were also asked to consider possible alternatives to library services, possible new services and the use their organization made or might make of information technology, issues that have been revisited to some extent in Chapter 3 of this book.

In addition, members of the team carried out focus group discussions with 144 representatives of staff at all levels. A senior member of the team also interviewed the heads of service, the chief executives and two key local politicians in each authority.

As indicated earlier, a wide range of attitudes was represented in the different members of the research team. This made it a very stimulating and rewarding experience for those of us involved. The final document is invariably a consensus, but it is one that points to a future which every member of the team believes could be exciting and worthwhile if the recommendations gain public, political and professional support.

The timing could have been better, but that was beyond our control. Although the government sees the report as an integral part of its overall review of public libraries, there must be a fear that the document may not be brought to life by an administration aware that it is close to the end of its own political life. Nevertheless, it contains much food for thought for the recently appointed Library Commission and a new political administration. It is to be hoped that members of the library profession will use the data in a positive way, and not just pick on the things with which they disagree.

The Bookseller, in its review of the work, commented that 'many of its recommendations will find instant favour in the public library community, while others rightly challenge that community to decide its stance in the face of the explosion of knowledge and of the methods of access to information' (*Bookseller* 1995). It remains to be seen whether that will be the case, but there is plenty in the report to enable the astute public library manager and the astute professional association to make a very good case for the kind of public library service most readers of this text would want to use and provide.

Appendix 2

Research questionnaire

 U N I V E R S I T Y   O F   S H E F F I E L D
DEPARTMENT OF INFORMATION STUDIES
Postal address: Western Bank, Sheffield S10 2TN
Location: Regent Court, 211 Portobello Street, Sheffield S1 4DP
Tel. 0114-2768555 Extns. 5080 & 5090 Direct Line 0114 282 5085 **Fax.**
0114-2780300
WWW. http://www.shef.ac.uk/uni/academic/I-M/is/home.html

15 September 1995

Dear Colleague

Public librarians have faced major changes in recent years. As you will be aware these changes include local government re-organization, competitive tendering, and the introduction of management techniques from the private sector.

I am currently undertaking research into the changing face of public library management and want to take account of the perceptions of leading practitioners. I would therefore be most grateful if you would complete the attached questionnaire so as to enable me to obtain an up-to-date picture of public library management in Britain.

The questionnaire, which makes use of previous work carried out by the Institute of Management, seeks your views, as a public library manager on:

- the factors driving managerial and organizational change
- the way these changes have affected you and your staff
- the way your organization has responded to change

Your answers will be treated in confidence and no individual will be identified in the final publication.

Please return the completed questionnaire by Friday October 20th 1995 to the above address. A reply paid envelope is enclosed for your convenience.

I should of course be happy to talk to you or your staff about this project at any time.

Thank you for taking part in this research,

Yours sincerely

Dr. Bob Usherwood
Reader in Librarianship and Information Studies.

THE CHANGING FACE OF PUBLIC LIBRARY MANAGEMENT

1.   These questions are concerned with the objectives of your library service. Please indicate the degree to which the following have increased or decreased over the past five years. *(Please tick one box only)*

	GREATLY INCREASED	INCREASED	STAYED THE SAME	DECREASED	GREATLY DECREASED
Focus on user needs	☐	☐	☐	☐	☐
Consultation with users about levels of service.	☐	☐	☐	☐	☐
Setting of output or outcome standards or measures	☐	☐	☐	☐	☐
Partnerships with other public bodies	☐	☐	☐	☐	☐
Partnerships with private sector organizations	☐	☐	☐	☐	☐
Provision of information to users about who is responsible for decisions	☐	☐	☐	☐	☐
Emphasis on eliminating discrimination in library provision to users	☐	☐	☐	☐	☐

2. These questions are concerned with library policies. Please indicate the degree to which the following have increased or decreased of the past five years. *(Please tick one box only)*

	GREATLY INCREASED	INCREASED	STAYED THE SAME	DECREASED	GREATLY DECREASED
The use of 'private sector' language to describe existing management techniques or approaches	☐	☐	☐	☐	☐
The use of 'private sector' management techniques or approaches	☐	☐	☐	☐	☐
The use of 'service level agreements' or 'contracts' to regulate internal transactions	☐	☐	☐	☐	☐
Emphasis on controlling spending	☐	☐	☐	☐	☐
Emphasis on efficiency of services	☐	☐	☐	☐	☐
Emphasis on effectiveness of services	☐	☐	☐	☐	☐
Emphasis on promoting staff development through training and other means	☐	☐	☐	☐	☐
Trying to create a 'learning organization' culture	☐	☐	☐	☐	☐

	GREATLY INCREASED	INCREASED	STAYED THE SAME	DECREASED	GREATLY DECREASED
The use of strategic planning systems	☐	☐	☐	☐	☐
The use of mission statements	☐	☐	☐	☐	☐
The introduction of more flexible organizational structures	☐	☐	☐	☐	☐
Removing managerial layers and creating flatter structures	☐	☐	☐	☐	☐
The use of performance-related pay	☐	☐	☐	☐	☐

2. (a)   If you have any comments on the policy changes that have taken place please add your comments below.

3.   These questions are concerned with the reasons for change. Please indicate the degree to which the following have been forces for change in the past five years.

	TO A GREAT EXTENT	TO SOME EXTENT BUT NOT A LARGE EXTENT	TO A SMALL EXTENT	TO NO EXTENT AT ALL
New policies imposed by central government	☐	☐	☐	☐
Government or other political pressure (other than legislation)	☐	☐	☐	☐
Pressure from new roles and types of management in similar organizations	☐	☐	☐	☐
Professional practice, ethics and values	☐	☐	☐	☐
Pressure from elected members	☐	☐	☐	☐
Consumer demands	☐	☐	☐	☐
Movement towards quality management	☐	☐	☐	☐
The Citizen's Charter or individual library charters	☐	☐	☐	☐
Need to reduce costs	☐	☐	☐	☐
Use of information technology	☐	☐	☐	☐

	TO A GREAT EXTENT	TO SOME EXTENT BUT NOT A LARGE EXTENT	TO A SMALL EXTENT	TO NO EXTENT AT ALL
Competition with non-public sector providers – private and voluntary	☐	☐	☐	☐
Concentration on core activities	☐	☐	☐	☐
Demographic trends and other social changes	☐	☐	☐	☐
Need to increase productivity or efficiency.	☐	☐	☐	☐

3. (a)   If you have any comments on the forces causing structural and managerial change in your organization please add them below.

4.   These questions are about culture, values and professional ethics. Please indicate the degree to which you feel the following have increased or decreased over the past five years

	GREATLY INCREASED	INCREASED	STAYED THE SAME	DECREASED	GREATLY DECREASED
Emphasis on 'public service ethos'	☐	☐	☐	☐	☐
Emphasis on public accountability	☐	☐	☐	☐	☐
Emphasis on 'professionalism' (that is, loyalty to the library profession not organization)	☐	☐	☐	☐	☐
Ability of managers to *recognize* 'right' ethical choices	☐	☐	☐	☐	☐
Ability of managers to *make* 'right' ethical choices	☐	☐	☐	☐	☐
Emphasis on commercial values as opposed to professional values.	☐	☐	☐	☐	☐

4.(a)   If you have any comments on the changes to the culture, value and ethics of your organization please add them below.

5.   These questions are about developing staff. Please indicate how satisfactory you
feel provision for staff development in your organization has been in the following areas.. (Please tick ONE box only in each line).

	VERY SATIS-FACTORY	SATISFACTORY	UNSATIS-FACTORY	VERY UNSATIS-FACTORY
Team working	☐	☐	☐	☐
Project management	☐	☐	☐	☐
Managing contracts	☐	☐	☐	☐
Using new technology	☐	☐	☐	☐
Managing decentralized budgets	☐	☐	☐	☐
Using performance monitoring systems	☐	☐	☐	☐
Using staff appraisal schemes	☐	☐	☐	☐
Dealing with political influences	☐	☐	☐	☐
Dealing with public relations and complaints	☐	☐	☐	☐
Developing management information systems	☐	☐	☐	☐

	VERY SATIS- FACTORY	SATISFACTORY	UNSATIS- FACTORY	VERY UNSATIS- FACTORY
Managing groups of professional staff	☐	☐	☐	☐
Formulating and implementing strategy	☐	☐	☐	☐
Marketing skills	☐	☐	☐	☐
Managing quality systems	☐	☐	☐	☐

5. (a)   If you have any comments on the support for staff development provided by your organization please add them below.

6.   These questions are concerned with your own power as the officer responsible for the library service. Please indicate the degree to which your own power has increased or decreased over the past five years.

	STRONGLY DECREASED	DECREASED	FAIRLY STABLE	INCREASED	STRONGLY INCREASED
Control your revenue budget	☐	☐	☐	☐	☐
Control your capital budget	☐	☐	☐	☐	☐
Move funds between different budget heads	☐	☐	☐	☐	☐
Retain (all or part) cost savings from efficiency improvements	☐	☐	☐	☐	☐
Raise and retain externally generated income	☐	☐	☐	☐	☐
Ability to resist political interference in operational decisions	☐	☐	☐	☐	☐

6. (a)   If you have any comments on changes in your own managerial power please add them below.

7.   These questions are about your own attitudes to change. If you have experienced any of the following over the past five years what has been your attitude towards them.

	VERY NEGATIVE	NEGATIVE	NEUTRAL	POSITIVE	VERY POSITIVE
Increase in personal job responsibilities	□	□	□	□	□
Reduction in management layers	□	□	□	□	□
Change to a 'private sector' organisational culture	□	□	□	□	□
Introduction of quality initiatives.	□	□	□	□	□
Management development programme	□	□	□	□	□
Greater use of team working	□	□	□	□	□
Competition with other providers	□	□	□	□	□
Service level agreements or contracts	□	□	□	□	□
Individual performance related payments	□	□	□	□	□
Appraisal systems	□	□	□	□	□

7. (a)   If you have any other comments on the way change has affected you please add them below.

More generally

8.   What do you consider to be the most significant changes in public library management in the past five years?

9.   What do you consider to be the limits of competitive tendering for public library services?

PLEASE TURN OVER

10.   To what extent should the private sector provide a model for performance measurement in public library services?

11.   Please state the type of local authority for which you work (e.g. English county, English metropolitan district, London borough, NI Education and Lib. Board, Scottish district, Welsh county etc.)

    ....

12.   Please indicate the political control of your local authority

    Conservative   ☐

    Labour   ☐

    Liberal/Democrat   ☐

    No overall control   ☐

    Other (please specify)   ☐

PLEASE TURN OVER

13.   Finally I should like to ask some questions about your own career development.

	General Admin or management	Functional or Technical professions (e.g. personnel, Legal, finance, IT)	Library/Information Professions	Other (Please specify)
Was your previous background in	☐	☐	☐	☐
Have you a qualification in	☐	☐	☐	☐

If yes please specify

_____

_____

	General Admin or management	Functional or Technical professions	Library/Information Professions	Other
Do you expect to gain a qualification in	☐	☐	☐	☐

	PUBLIC SECTOR	PRIVATE SECTOR	VOLUNTARY SECTOR	OTHER
How long (*in years*) have you worked in	☐	☐	☐	☐
Where do you expect to be working in five years' time?	☐	☐	☐	☐

PLEASE TURN OVER

14.   Would you be willing to be interviewed as part of the follow-up research to the questionnaire?

                         Yes   ☐

                         No   ☐

Please give your details below. (This will help me contact you if required. However, please leave this section blank if you prefer)

Name: ....

Organization:...

Address:..

....

....

Telephone..

Fax...

Thank you for your cooperation
Your reply will be treated in *strictest confidence*

Please return the questionnaire by **Friday October 20 1995** to

Dr R. Usherwood
Reader
Department of Information Studies
University of Sheffield
Sheffield
S10 2TN

Bibliography

Adam Smith Institute (1986) *Ex Libris*.

Alban-Metcalf, B. (1989), 'What motivates managers: an investigation by gender and sector of employment', *Public administration*, **67** (Spring), 95–108.

American Library Association (1986), *Freedom and equality of access to information*, (Lacy Report), Chicago, American Library Association.

Amis, M. (1995), *The information*, London, Flamingo.

Anstice, I. (1994), *Public attitudes towards the financing of public libraries. A study submitted in partial fulfilment of the requirements for the degree of Master of Arts in Librarianship*, University of Sheffield.

Argyle, M. (1990), *Bodily communication*, London, Routledge.

Arnold, B. and Usherwood, B. (1976), 'The library in the cultural framework' in Harrison, K. C., *Prospects for British librarianship*, Library Association.

Arvidsson, R. (1986), 'Performance evaluation' in Kaufman, F. X. *et al.* (eds.), *Guidance , control and evaluation in the public domain*, Berlin, de Gruyter.

Aslib (1995), *Review of the public library service in England and Wales for the Department of National Heritage. Final Report*, London, Aslib.

Association of County Councils (1980), *The feasibility of charging for public library lending services, report to the Recreation Committee*, 10 June.

Association of London Authorities, Arts and Recreation Committee (1987), *Library services in ALA boroughs. A report on the range of issues affecting service delivery in inner city libraries, including recommendations for implementation of the service*.

Audit Commission (1990), *We can't go on meeting like this. The changing role of local authority members*, London, HMSO.

Audit Commission (1992), *The Citizen's Charter performance indicators*, London, HMSO.

Audit Commission (1993), *Putting quality on the map*, London, HMSO.

Baddeley, S. (1988), 'Political sensitivity in public managers' in Young, K. *et al.*, *Managing at the political/professional interface*, University of Birmingham, Public Service Management Centre, 23–39.

Bains (1972),*The new local authorities: management and structure*, London, HMSO.

Bajaria, H. J. (1995), 'Effective TQM implementation: critical issues' in Kanji, G. K. (ed.), *Total quality management. Proceedings of the first world congress*, London, Chapman and Hall, 128–46.

Baker, B. N. (1984), 'When the left appoints its own', *Daily Telegraph*, 3 February, 18.

Barnett, A. (1996), 'Conjuring trick of private finance', *The Observer* Business Section, 7 April, 5.

Barrett, S. and Fudge, C. (1981), *Policy and action*, London, Methuen.

Baskerville, R. and Smithson, S. (1995), 'Information technology and new organisational forms: choosing chaos over panaceas', *European journal of information systems*, **4**, 66–73.

Becker, G. S. (1996), 'Why Europe is drowning in joblessness', *Business week*, 8 April, 7.

Betts, D. (1985), 'Stock management' in Harris, C. and Clifford, B. (eds.), *Public libraries: reappraisal and restructuring*, London, Rossendale.

Billington, M. (1993), 'I just do an arts show, a little radio and write books', *The Guardian*, 27 November.

Blake, D. J., Frederick, W. C. and Myers, M.S. (1976), *Social audit: evaluating the impact of corporate programmes*, Praeger.

Blanchard, K. H. (1994), *The one minute manager*, London.

Boddy, M. and Fudge, C. (eds.) (1984), *Local socialism? Labour councils and new left alternatives*, London, Macmillan.

Bone, C. (1993), *Modern quality management manual*, London.

Booker, D. (1993), *Twice paid; user pays and public libraries*, Adelaide, Auslib Press.

Borrowed time? The future of public libraries in the United Kingdom (1993), Bournes Green, Comedia.

Bottomley, V. (1995), The public library service. Virginia Bottomley sets out libraries key functions. News Release DNH 255/95.

Bottomley, V. (1996), Competitive tendering for public library service. News Release DNH 110/96.

Boynton, J. (1986), *Job at the top; the chief executive in local government*, London, Longman.

Bradbury, M. (1978), *Eating people is wrong*, London, Arrow Books.

Brindle, D. (1996), 'The internal market, warps and all', *The Guardian* Society 24 April, 6.

British social attitudes the 11th report (1994), Aldershot, Dartmouth Publishing Company for Social and Community Planning Research.

British Standards Institution (1987–91), BS 4778 *Quality vocabulary*, 3 parts, Hemel Hempstead, BSI.

British Standards Institution (1991), BS5750 Part 8: Quality management and quality system elements, Part 2: Guidelines for services, Hemel Hempstead, BSI.

British Standards Institution (1992), BS7850 Total quality management, Part 1: Guide to management principles, Part 2: Guide to quality improvement methods, Hemel Hempstead, BSI.

Brooke, P. (1994), quoted in Department of National Heritage Libraries Division *Newsbrief,* 1 February.

Brown, A. (1995), 'Human factors: the problems of integrating people and technology in the workplace', *On the horizon,* 3 (4), April/May, 1–2, 5–6.

Brown, J. and Sime, J. (1981), 'A methodology for accounts' in Brenner, M. (ed.), *Social method and social life,* London Academic Press, 159–88.

Budge, H. D. (1971), 'The public library service' in Rose, B. (ed.), *The councillor's work,* London, Charles Knight & Co Ltd, 83–7.

Burge, S. (1995), 'Performance related pay and government libraries', *Personnel training and education,* 11 (3), 3–6.

Cabinet Office, Office of the Minister for the Civil service (1988), *Service to the public,* Occasional paper, London, HMSO.

Carlin, J. (1996), 'Guru of 'downsizing' admits he got it all wrong', *Independent on Sunday,* 12 May, 1.

CCTA (1994), 'BPR in the public sector. Meeting the challenge of change in government', *CCTA business management,* December.

Centre for Information Quality Management (1994), *Quality of data in online and CD-ROM databases,* 2nd report, CIQM.

Cheese, J. (1994), Letter, *Public library journal,* 9 (1), 32.

Cheshire County Council (nd), *The Cheshire values* (mimeo supplied to author).

CIPFA (1996), *Public library statistics/1994–95 Actuals,* London.

The Citizen's Charter – raising the standard (1991), Cmnd 1599, London, HMSO.

Circle of State Librarians (1992), *Developing quality in libraries,* London, HMSO.

Cleese, J. and others (1994), 'Alarm over public library changes', Letter, *The Times,* 16 May, 17.

Clouston, E. (1991), 'Private sector binmen junk their old image', *The Guardian,* 30 July.

Cochrane, A. (1993), *Whatever happened to local government,* Buckingham, Open University Press.

Cole, N. and Usherwood, B., *Library and stock management policies, statements and philosophies,* (in press).

Community leadership and representation: unlocking the potential (1993), The Report of the Working Party on the Internal Management of Local Authorities in England, London, HMSO.

Corbett, E. V. (1979), 'Leisure or liability?' in Usherwood, B., *Libraries and leisure,* Association of Assistant Librarians, South East Division.

Cram, J. (1995), 'Indigenous roots and local bluebirds: managing libraries for effectiveness in a new society', *Kwaznaplis,* 1 (5), 3–10.

Crosby, P. (1979), *Quality is free,* New York, McGraw-Hill.

Cunningham, G. (1991), speaking on 'The World at One', BBC Radio Four, (precise date not known).

Curley, A. (1989), Paper given to the IFLA Conference 1989.

Curley, A. (1994), 'Introduction' in Gertzog, A. and Beckerman, E., *Administration of the public library*, Metuchen, NJ, The Scarecrow Press Inc.

Curry, M. A. (1993), *A comparison of the roles and attitudes of Canadian and British public library directors in dealing with intellectual freedom issues*. PhD thesis, Department of Information Studies, University of Sheffield.

Curtis, M. (1993), 'Quality assurance in Kent', *Public libraries journal*, **7** (2), Jan–Feb.

Davies, A. and Kirkpatrick, I. (1995), 'Performance indicators, bureaucratic control and the decline of professional autonomy; the case of academic librarians', in Kirkpatrick, I. and Lucio, M. M. (eds.) (1995), *The politics of quality in the public sector*, London, Routledge, 84–107.

Davies, C. (1995), *Hearts and minds: the role in commercial organisational restructuring*. (Paper distributed via the Internet.)

Dearlove, J. (1973), *The politics of policy in local government*, Cambridge, Cambridge University Press.

Deming, W. E. (1986), *Out of the crisis*, Cambridge, MA., MIT Centre for Advanced Engineering Study.

Department of Trade and Industry (1996), *Competitiveness forging ahead* hhtp://www.publications.hmso.gov.uk/hmso/document/dti-comp/chap5.htm

Dudley, E. (1991), 'Libraryland: those twentieth-century blues', *Library Association record*, **93** (1/2), 21.

Eastell, C. (1994), *Compulsory competitive tendering. The right thing for the public library service? An investigation of the view of chief librarians. A study submitted in partial fulfilment of the requirements for the degree of Master of Arts in Librarianship*, University of Sheffield.

Edgar, D. (1991), 'Are you being served?', *Marxism today*, May 28.

Elcock, H. (1994), 'The parlous state of British democracy', *Public management and money*, **14** (4).

Elcock, H. (1996), 'Strategic management' in Farnham, D. and Horton, S. (eds.), *Managing the new public services*,2nd edn, Basingstoke, Macmillan Press.

Evans, M. (1996a), Foreword to *Shelf talk: promoting literature in public libraries*, distributed by the Poetry Society.

Evans, M. (1996b), Address to Library Association Council 12 June.

Evans, M. K. (1991), *All change? Public library management strategies for the 1990s*, London, Taylor Graham.

Faith, N. (1996), 'Imprisoned by a grand delusion', *Independent on Sunday* Business, 8 January, 6.

Farnham, D. and Horton, S. (eds.) (1993), *Managing the new public services*, Basingstoke, Macmillan Press.

Farnham, D. and Horton, S. (eds.) (1996a), *Managing the new public services*, 2nd edn, Basingstoke, Macmillan Press.

Farnham, D. and Horton, S. (1996), 'Public service managerialism: a review and evaluation', in Farnham, D. and Horton, S. (eds.), *Managing the new public services*, 2nd edn, Basingstoke, Macmillan Press.

Flynn, N. (1993), *Public sector management*, 2nd edn, London, Harvester.

Fontaine, S. (1975), *Report to the Council on Library Resources. Public relations in public libraries.*

Foster, M. and Whittle, S. (1989), 'The quality management maze', *Total quality management*, **1** (3), 143–8.

Fowler, R. (1994), 'Is Thatcher's arts revolution over?', *Sunday Times*, 18 December, 8.

Frankena, F. and Frankena, J. (1986), 'The politics of expertise and the role of the librarian', *Behavioural and social science librarian*, Fall/Winter, 39.

Freely, M. (1996), 'Monster raving loony bosses', *The Guardian* (Second Section), June 10, 6–7.

Frohman, M. (1994), 'Re-mything management', *Industry week*, 21 May, v.243 (6), 21–3.

From vision to action. Info-society 2000. Statement to Parliament on 'Info-Society 2000' and IT Political Action Plan 1995 (1995), Denmark, Ministry of Research and Information Technology, 39.

Galbraith, J. K. (1979), 'Are public libraries against liberty?', *American libraries*, **10** (8), 482–6.

Galbraith, J. K. (1994), 'Towards a new world deal', *The Guardian* Second Front, 26 January, 2–3.

Garrod, P. and Evans, M. K. (in press), *Towards library excellence: Best practice benchmarking in the library and information sector*, A British Library Research and Development Report.

Gaster, L. (1995), *Quality in public services*, Buckingham Open University Press.

Gerard, D. (1988), *Shrieking silence: a library landscape*, Metuchen, NJ, Scarecrow Press.

Getting closer to the public (1987), Luton, Local Government Training Board.

Giappiconi, T. (1995), 'Library evaluation and public policy: a French view', *Journal of librarianship and information science*, **27** (2), 99–108.

Glenn, T. (nd), Leadership TQM BB5 301 585 1164 (Internet discussion group).

The Glue that binds (1996), London, Public Management Foundation: MORI.

Goodson-Wickes, C. (1984), *The new corruption*, London, Centre for Policy Studies.

Gosling, P. (1993), 'Adam Smith's revolution', *The Independent on Sunday*, 11 April, 27.

Goulding, A. (1996), *Managing change for library support staff*, Aldershot, Avebury.

Govan, J. F. (1988), 'The creeping invisible hand: entrepreneurial librarianship', *Library journal*, **113** (1), 35–8.

Gray, R. (1995), 'Social and environmental accounting research', *Briefings from the GEC Programme*, GEC Programme Office, University of Sussex.

Green, S. S. (1876), 'Personal relations between librarians and readers', *Library journal*, 1 October, 74–81.

Greenhalgh L. and Worpole, K. with Landry. C. (1995), *Libraries in a world of cultural change*, London, UCL Press.

Greenwood, T. (1891), *Public libraries, a history of the movement and a manual for the organisation and management of rate supported libraries*, 4th edn, Cassell.

Guest, D. (1992), 'Right enough to be dangerously wrong; an analysis of the *In search of excellence* phenomenon', in. Salaman, G. et al. (eds.) (1992), *Human resource strategies*, London, Sage.

Gunn, L. (1987), 'Perspectives on public management', in Kooiman, J. and Eliassen, K. A. (eds.), *Managing public organizations. Lessons from contemporary European experience*, London, Sage.

Gyford, J. (1985), *The politics of local socialism*, London, George Allen & Unwin.

Gyford, J., Leach, S. and Game, C. (1989), *The changing politics of local government*, London, Unwin Hyman.

Haigh, R. H. and Morris, D. S. (1995), 'The development of a generic model for the implementation of TQM', in Kanji, G. K. (ed.) (1995), *Total quality management. Proceedings of the first world congress*, London, Chapman Hall, 85–94.

Haines, M., 'Continuous quality improvement at the King's Fund Centre', in HERTIS (1993), *Total quality management. The Information Business: Key Issue 92*, HERTIS Information and Research, 46–56.

Halliday, J. (1992), 'Fee or free: a new perspective on the economics of information', *Canadian library journal*, **48** (5), 327–33.

Halmos, P. (1970), *The personal service society*, London, Constable.

Harris, R. (1988), 'The information needs of battered women', *Reference quarterly*, **28**, 62–70.

Harris, R. (1992), 'Information technology and the deskilling of librarians', (mimeo of paper to appear in *the Encyclopaedia of library and information science*).

Harvey, J. B. (1988), 'The Abilene paradox: the management of agreement', *Organizational dynamics*, Summer, 17–43.

Hassell, N. (1993), 'Private virtues of public service', *Management today*, February, 58–61.

Haywood, T. (1995), *Info-rich info-poor: access and exchange in the global information society*, London, Bowker Saur.

Heaton, S. and Brown J. M. (1995), 'Staff perceptions of incentives and hurdles to the use of technology', *Computers in libraries*, **15** (2), 28–31.

Heery, M. (1995), 'Managerialism – does it have to be for or against?', *Library manager*, (4), February, 28.

Heinitz, C. (1993), 'The public library review. An elected member's view', *Public library journal*, **8** (6), 161–6.

Hicks, D. (1995), *Research project to develop and implement a proposal for an accredited literature module for librarianship courses*, London, Arts Council of England.

Hines, B. (1983), *Unfinished business*, London, Michael Joseph.

Hoadley, I. B. (1995), 'Customer service? Not really', *College and research libraries news*, **56** (3), 175–6.

Hoggart, R. (1995a), 'Why treat us like dimwits?', *Independent on Sunday*, 19 February, 21.

Hoggart, R. (1995b), *The way we live now*, London, Chatto & Windus.

Hoggart, R. (1991), 'A public library is not a burger bar', *Independent on Sunday*, 20 June, 22.

Hopkins, L. (1994), 'Local government review: the implications for central support services', *Journal of the National Acquisitions Group*, **32** (2), 20–6.

Hoover, K. and Plant, R. (1989), *Conservative capitalism in Britain and the United States: a critical appraisal*, London, Routledge.

Hughill, B. (1995), 'Children to jump library queue', *The Observer*, 5 March, 7.

Hughill, B. and Gold, K. (1996), 'Selective evidence of "schools spin doctor" ', *The Observer*, 5 May, 4.

Hutton, W. (1996a), *The state we're in*, London, Vintage.

Hutton, W. (1996b), 'A nation knocked over by the domino effect', *The Observer review*, 23 June, 3.

Ignatieff, M. (1988), 'The tide will turn', *The Guardian*, 4 April.

Ignatieff, M. (1991), 'Gradgrind rules in the public libraries', *The Observer*, 2 June, 19.

Irving, A. (1992), 'Quality in academic libraries: how shall we know it?', *Aslib information*, **20** (6), June.

Irving, W. (1824), *Tales of a traveller*, London, John Murray.

Isaac-Henry, K., Painter, C. and Barnes, C. (eds.) (1993), *Management in the public sector: challenges and change*, London, Chapman & Hall.

Jackson, P. M. and Palmer, B. (1992), *Developing performance monitoring in public sector organisations. A management guide*, Management Centre, University of Leicester.

Janis, I. L. (1968), *Victims of groupthink; a psychological study of foreign policy decisions and fiascos*, Boston, MA., Houghton Mifflin.

Jast, L. S. (1935), 'Public libraries' in Laski, H. J., Jennings, W. I. and Robson, W. A. (eds.), *A century of municipal progress 1835–1935*, London, Allen & Unwin, 244–59.

Javerski, B. (1996), 'Free markets crying in the wilderness', *Business week*, 8 April, 24.

Joint Funding Councils' Libraries Review Group Report (1993), Libraries Review Group, Education Funding Council Bristol, HFCE

Jones, D. (1995), 'Citizen's Charter – performance indicators – a view from Hackney', *BURISA*, **118**, 7–9.

Jones, G. W. (1973), 'The functions and organization of councillors', *Public administration*, **51** (2), 135–46.

Jones, G. W. and Stewart, J. D. (1985), *The case for local government*, 2nd edn, London, Allen & Unwin.

Jordan. T. (1994), 'Give us a byte', *The Scotsman*, 17 November, 17.

Juran, J. M. (1979), *Quality control handbook*, 3rd edn, New York, McGraw Hill.

Kanji, G. K. (ed.) (1995), *Total quality management. Proceedings of the first world congress*, London, Chapman & Hall.

Kano, N. (1995), 'Upsizing the organisation by attractive quality creation', in Kanji, G. K. (ed.) (1995) *Total quality management. Proceedings of the first world congress*, London, Chapman & Hall.

Kanter, R. M. (1983), *The change masters*, London, Allen & Unwin.

Kanter, R. M. (1985), 'Managing the human side of change', *Management review*, April, 52–6.

Kaufmann, G. (1995), House of Commons debate on the Citizen's Charter, 13 February.

Kendall, M. (1992), 'Section 11 changes in funding criteria: the implications for public library services for black and minority ethnic groups', *Public library journal*, **7** (2), 37–40.

Kerley, R. (1994), *Managing in local government*, Basingstoke, Macmillan.

Kinnell, M. (ed.) (1991), *Managing fiction in libraries*, London, Library Association.

Kinnell, M. (1996), 'Managing in a corporate culture', in Kinnell, M. and Sturges, P. (eds.), *Continuity and innovation in the public library. The development of a social institution*, London, Library Association.

Kinnell, M. and MacDougall, J. (1993), *Meeting the marketing challenge: strategies for public libraries and leisure services,* London, Taylor Graham

Kirkpatrick, I. and Lucio, M. M. (1995), *The politics of quality in the public sector*, London, Routledge.

Knowles, R. S. B. (1988), *Effective management in local government*, Cambridge, ICSA Publishing.

Kooiman, J. and Eliassen, K. A. (eds.) (1987), *Managing public organizations. Lessons from contemporary European experience*, London, Sage.

Kouses, J. M. and Mico, P. R. (1979), 'Domain theory', *Journal of applied behavioural science*, **15** (4), 449–69.

KPMG Peat Marwick (1994), *DNH study contracting-out in public libraries. Draft report by KPMG and CPI for public consultation.*

KPMG (1995), *DNH study: contracting-out in public libraries*, KPMG & CPI.

Labdon, P. (1991), 'Acquiring adult fiction', in Kinnell, M. (ed.), *Managing fiction in libraries*, London, Library Association, 34–47.

Labour Party (1991), *Opportunity, quality, accountability – the better way for local government*, London, Labour Party.

Labour Party (1995), *Labour communicating Britain's future* (Internet version).

Laffin, M. and Young, K. (1990), *Professionalism in local government: change and challenge*, Harlow, Longman.

LAMSAC [Local Authorities Management Services and Computer Committee] (nd), *The information needs of elected members*, London, LAMSAC.

Lancaster, F. W. (1993), *If you want to evaluate your library . . .* 2nd edn, London, Library Association.

Landry, C. (1993), *Fundamental dilemmas for public libraries: Working paper Four*, Stroud, Comedia.

Law, D. (1996), 'A MAN for all reasons?', *Ariadne*, 2 March.

Lawson, M. (1996), 'Crowding out the author', *The Guardian*, 6 February,12.

Lawton, A. and Rose, A. (1994), *Organisation and management in the public sector*, 2nd edn, London, Pitman.

Levy, P. and Usherwood, B. (1992), *People skills: Interpersonal skills training for library and information work*, (Library & Information Research Report 88), London, British Library.

Library Association(1991), *Comments of the LA in regard to the extension of compulsory competitive tendering to public library services*, London, Library Association.

Library Association (1993), *A Charter for Public Libraries*, London, Library Association.

Library Association (1994a), *Local government reorganisation in England.* [A briefing paper on the effects of Local Government Review on public library services], London, Library Association.

Library Association (1994b), *The recruitment and training of library and information staff from cultural minorities*, London, Library Association.

Library Association (1995) *Model statement of standards* London, L.A.

Line, M. (1980), 'Ignoring the user: how, when and why', in *The nationwide provision and use of information. Aslib, IIS, LA Joint Conference 15–19 September 1980 Sheffield. Proceedings*, London, Library Association.

Local Government Training Board (1987b), *Politicians and professionals – the changing management of local government*, Luton, Local Government Training Board.

Lomer, M. and Rogers, S. (1983), *The public library and the local authority.* University of Birmingham, Institute of Local Government Studies. (British Library Research & Development Report, No. 5738).

Lovell, R. (1994), *Managing change in the new public sector*, Harlow, Longman.

Loughborough University (1994), *L.I.S.U. Annual library statistics 1994*, Loughborough, L.I.S.U.

Malley, I. (1990), *Censorship and libraries* (Viewpoints in Library and Information Science, no 5), London, Library Association.

Marquand, D. (1993), 'Labour's new model army', *The Guardian*, 26 May, 18.

Martines, L. (1993), 'British Library's words of wisdom', Letter, *The Times*, 10 September.

McCarthy, A., Shaw, K., Fenwick, J. and Foreman, A. (1992), *Compulsory competitive tendering in local government. An annotated bibliography*, Humberside, Earlsgate Press.

McGregor, D. (1960), *The human side of enterprise*, New York, McGraw Hill.

McKee, B. (1987), *Public libraries into the 1990s?* , Newcastle-Under-Lyme, AAL Publishing.

McKevitt, D. and Lawton, A. (eds.) (1994), *Public sector management. Theory, critique and practice*, London, Sage, in association with the Open University.

McNicol, I. (1995), quoted in 'Bottomley rejects library CCT', LGC Net. 28 07.

Meikle, J. (1996), 'Reading the bottom line', *The Guardian* Society, 21 February, 25.

Midwinter, A. and McVicar, M. (1993), 'Population size and functional efficiency in public library authorities: the statistical evidence', *Journal of librarianship and information science,* **25** (4), 187–96.

Midwinter, A. and McVicar, M. (1994), *The size and efficiency debate: public library authorities in time of change*, London, Library Association.

Milner, E. Kinnell, M. and Usherwood, B. (1994), 'Quality management: the public library debate', *Public library journal*, **9** (6), 151–7.

Milner, E., Evans, M. and Usherwood, B. (in press), *Quality management in public library services: The right approach?* (British Library Research and Development Department).

Miller, L. M. (nd) quoted by Glenn, T., *Leadership*, TQM BBS 301 585 1164 (Internet discussion group).

Mintzberg, H. (1980), *The nature of managerial work*, Englewood Cliffs, NJ, Prentice Hall.

Mistry, V. and Usherwood, B. (1995), 'Total quality management, British Standard accreditation, Investors in people and academic libraries', *Information research news*, **6** (3), November, 11–22.

Monroe, P. A. (1987), 'Managing the political process: the local politician's viewpoint'. Paper given to London & Home Counties Branch of the Library Association, one-day course: 'Managing the political process: the neglected area of library management', 13 May (mimeo from author).

Morgan, P. and Potter, C. (1995), 'Professional cultures and paradigms of quality in health care', in Kirkpatrick, I. and Lucio, M. M., *The politics of quality in the public sector*, London, Routledge.

Morgan, W. W. (1996), Letter, *Business week*, 8 April, 4.

Morris, D. (1994), *The human zoo*, London, Vintage.

Murray, P. and Letch, R. (1987), *Getting closer to the public*, Luton, LGTB.

National Consumer Council (1977), *The fourth right of citizenship*, London, National Consumer Council.

Naughton, J. (1995), 'Notes on life, liberty and the pursuit of power. Turn on, tune in, cop out', *The Observer review*, 22 December, 13.

Naughton, J. (1996), 'Notes on life, liberty and the pursuit of power. Crawling along the bottom line', *The Observer review*, 7 January, 12.

Newhard, R. D. (1993), 'Technology and the potential demise of public libraries'. (Message posted on the Internet 21 June).

Nicholson, V. (1987), 'The political dimension', in Coleman, P. M. (ed.), *Libraries and the arts in action or inaction? Proceedings of the Sheffield Conference November 1985*, Sheffield City Libraries, 90–5.

Nilsson, E. (1994), Editorial, *Scandinavian public library quarterly*, **27** (1), 3.

OECD (1992), *Public management development: update*, Paris, OECD.

Office of Arts and Libraries (1990), *Keys to success: performance indicators for public libraries*, London, HMSO.

Office of Arts and Libraries (1991), *Setting objectives for public library services* (Library Information Series 19), London, HMSO.

Osborne, D. and Gaebler, T. (1992), *Reinventing government: How the entrepreneurial spirit is transforming the public sector*, Reading, MA, Addison-Wesley.

Osborne, J. (1960), *Look back in anger*, London, Faber and Faber.

Owen, D., 'Innovation during recession', in Harris, C. and Clifford, B. (eds.) (1985), *Public libraries; reappraisal and restructuring*, London, Rossendale.

Owen, D. (1995), 'An idealist's charter for public libraries', *New library world*, **96** (1120), 6–15.

Page, R. (1996), 'Locking horns with the welfare foe', Letter, *Times higher education supplement*, 24 May, 12.

Palmer, A. (1996), 'Marketing in an environment of social responsibility', *Academic newsletter. Marketing*, McGraw Hill. [Publisher's promotional flyer]

Parker, M. and Jary, D. (1995), 'The McUniversity: organization, management and academic subjectivity', *Organization*, **2** (2), 319–38.

Parsons, S. (1988), 'Economic principles in the public and private sectors', *Policy and politics,* **16** (1), 29–39.

Parston, G. (1994), 'Dangers in dogma', *The Guardian*, 10 August, 15.

Percy-Smith, J. and Sanderson, I. (1992), *Understanding local needs*, London, Institute for Public Policy Research.

Perry, J. L. and Kraemer, K. L. (eds.) (1983), *Public management; public and private perspectives*, California, Mayfield.

Peters, T. (1988), *Thriving on chaos*, London, Macmillan.

Peters, T. J. and Waterman, R. H. (1982), *In search of excellence: lessons from America's best run companies*, New York, Harper & Row.

Pfeffer, N. and Coote, A. (1991), *Is quality good for you?* , Bristol, Institute for Public Policy Research.

Pollitt, C. (1988), 'Bringing consumers into performance measurement: concepts, consequences and constraints', *Policy and politics*, **16** (2), 1–11.

Pollitt, C. (1993), *Managerialism and the public services*, 2nd edn, Oxford, Blackwell.

Porter, H. (1995), 'Corporate punishment', *The Guardian*, 19 June, 12–13.

Porter. L. (1992), *Quality initiatives in British Library and Information Services* (BLR&D Report 6105), London, British Library.

Portrait of change (1996), Luton, Local Government Training Board.

Potter, D. (1993), 'Occupying powers', *The Guardian*, 28 August, 21.

Potter, D. (1994), *Seeing the blossom. Two interviews and a lecture*, London, Faber & Faber.

Potter, J. (1988), 'Consumerism and the public sector: how well does the coat fit?', *Public administration*, (66), Summer, 149–64.

Powledge, T. (1994), 'Maryland opens first cyber-library', *The Independent*, 8 July.

'Prisoners of Tory mistrust' (1995), *Independent on Sunday*, 22 October, 20.

Pritchard, N. and Usherwood, B. (1989), *Publicly-funded libraries expenditure in the private sector. A study of Yorkshire and Humberside libraries*, Yorkshire and Humberside Branch of the Library Association.

Proctor, R. V., Sobczyk, G. and Usherwood, B. (in press), 'What do people do when their library closes down?', *LIRG news*.

'Public library review urges growth, higher standards' (1995), *The bookseller*, 2 June.

'Quality Street may be a dead end' (1994), *Management decision*, September, v.**32** (5), 12.

Ranson, S. and Stewart, J. (1994), *Management for the public domain: Enabling the learning society*, London, St. Martin's Press.

Rawlinson, N. (1986), 'The approach to collection management at Baltimore County public library', in Serebnick, J, (ed.), *Collection management in public libraries*, Chicago, American Library Association, 76–80.

Rawlinson, N. (1981), 'Give em what they want!', *Library journal*, **106** (20), 2188–90.

Reid, J. (1982), *Education and training for community information and advice work*, Sheffield, University of Sheffield Department of Information Studies. (Occasional publications series No 1).

Reuter, M. E. (1991), *The influence of technology on women librarians' and library assistants' work experience*, PhD, State University of New York at Albany.

Roberts, A. M. (1993), Letter, *Times higher educational supplement*, 30 April, 13.

Roberts, N. (1986), 'Service performance and consumerism', *CRUS news*, 25 July, 8–11.

Roberts, N. (1991), 'A profession in crisis', *Library Association record*, **93** (7), July 450–53.

Roberts, N. (1994), Review of Moon, E. (1993), *A desire to learn: selected writings*, Metuchen, NJ, Scarecrow Press, in *Journal of information and library research*, **6** (1/2), 77–9.

Rogers, E. M. (1962), *Diffusion of innovations*, New York, Free Press.

Rogers, S. (1990), *Performance management in local government*, Harlow, Longman and Local Government Training Board.

Ruse, D., *Public libraries: the story so far . . .* HERTIS, 1993, 31–7.

Rutter, L. (1980), *The essential community; local government in the year 2000*, Washington, International City Management Association.

Samuel, R. (1992), 'No mythic golden age', *New statesman & society*, 5, 6 March, 16–17.

Samuelson, P. (1954), 'The pure theory of public expenditure', *Review of economics and statistics*, **36** (Nov), 387–9.

Sanderson, I. (ed.) (1992), *Management of quality in local government*, London, Longman.

Sapir, E. (1971), 'Language', in Thompson, K. and Tunstall, J, (eds.) (1971), *Sociological perspectives*, Harmondsworth, Penguin.

Savage, E. (1942), *The librarian and his committee*, London, Grafton.

Schein, E. H. (1985), *Organizational culture and leadership*, San Francisco, Jossey-Bass.

Sharpe, L. J. and Newton, K. (1984), *Does politics matter? The determinants of public policy*, Oxford, Clarendon Press.

Shelf Talk (1996), *Promoting literature in public libraries*. Distributed by the Poetry Society.

Simmons, M. (1995), 'Gummer blows cold on wind of change', *The Guardian*, 3 March, 5.

Simon, H. (1957), *Administrative behaviour*, New York, Macmillan.

Slovic, P. et al. (1982), 'Facts and fears: understanding perceived risk', in Schwing, R. and Albers, W. A. (eds.), *Societal risk assessment. How safe is safe enough*, New York, Plenum.

Smith, J. (1982), 'Living in interesting times: the management of change', in *Scottish Library Association 68th Annual Conference Proceedings. Preparing for change.*

Snape, R. (1995), *Leisure and the rise of the public library*, London, Library Association.

Social Trends (1993), Central Statistical Office.

Sproat, I. (1993), Paper to Public Libraries Authority Conference, Torquay.

St. Clair, G. (1994a), 'The times they are a changin . .', *Library manager*, 2 December, 12–15.

St. Clair, G. (1994b), *Power and influence: enhancing information services within the organization*, London, Bowker Saur.

Stevens, E. (1984), 'Channel Islands transition from subscription to free service', *Library Association record*, **86** (5), May, 212–4.

Stewart, J. (1983), The role of the public library and information services in an age of uncertainty. *Proceedings of the Public Library Authorities Conference 1983.* Public Libraries Group, The Library Association, 1–6.

Stewart, J. (1988), *The role of councillors in the management of local authorities*, London, Audit Commission.

Stewart, J. and Ranson, S. (1988), 'Management in the public domain', *Public money and management*, Spring–Summer, 13–19.

Stewart, J. and Walsh, K. (1989), *The search for quality*, Luton, Local Government Training Board.

Stewart, J. and Walsh, K. (1992), 'Change in the management of public services', *Public administration*, Winter, 499–518.

Stewart, J. and Walsh, K. (1994), 'Performance and measurement when performance can never be finally defined', *Public money and management*, **14** (2), 45–9.

Stoakley, R. (1983), 'Presenting the library service: the political management of libraries', in Usherwood, B. (ed.), *Professional persuasion. Library public relations and promotion. Proceedings of the AAL Weekend Conference, Harrogate, May 6–8 1983*, London, AAL,18–22.

'The straining of quality' (1995), *The economist*, 14 January, 65–6.

Stroud, G. and Usherwood, B. (1995), 'Towards a model statement of standards for public library services', *Public library journal*, **10** (1), 1–4.

Sumsion, J. (1993), *Practical performance indicators –1992: Documenting the Citizen's Charter consultation for UK Public Libraries with examples of PIs and surveys in use*, Library and Information Statistics Unit, Dept. of Information and Library Studies, Loughborough University of Technology.

Swan, J. (1990), *Fundraising for the small public library; a how-to-do-it manual for librarians*, New York, Neal-Schuman.

Talbot, C. (1994), *Reinventing public management. A survey of public managers' reactions to change*, Corby, Institute of Management.

Tawney, R. H. (1975), *Equality*, 4th rev edn, London, Unwin Books.

Taylor, A. (1993), *Long overdue: a library reader*, Edinburgh and London, Library Association in conjunction with Mainstream Publishing.

Taylor, F. W. (1911), *Principles of scientific management*, New York, Harper Press.

Taylor, I. (1996), quoted in 'Three keys to open global superhighway , says Ian Taylor', DTI Press notice P/96/359.

Taylor, L.(1993), 'Quality Street column', *New statesman*, 22 October, v.6 (275), 25.

Thompson, A. H. (1975), *Censorship in public libraries*, Epping, Bowker.

'Tirisias' (1975), 'Libraries in leisure', *Recreation management*, December/January.

Toffler, A. (1970), *Future shock*, New York, Random House.

Totterdell, B. and Bird, J. (1976), *The effective library. Report of the Hillingdon Project on public library effectiveness*, M. Redfern (ed.), London, Library Association.

Tullis, S. E. (1995), Summation of Peter Young's remarks to Federal Depository Conference (Public Libraries and the Internet/NII) provided to multiple recipients of list GOVDOC April 14

Tully, M. (1993), 'An ill wind of change on the airwaves', *The Guardian*, 14 July, 6.

Tversky, A. and Kahneman, B. (1982), 'Judgement under uncertainty: heuristic and biases', *Science,* 185.

Underwood, P. (1990), *Managing change in libraries and information services*, London, Library Association.

UNESCO Public Library Manifesto 1994 (1995), *IFLA public library news. Newsletter of the Section of Public Libraries,* January 1995, Issue No 12.

Usherwood, B. (ed.) (1979), *Libraries and leisure*, Association of Assistant Librarians, South East Division.

Usherwood, B. (1980), 'Professional values in a bureaucratic structure', *Library review,* (29), Spring, 8–14.

Usherwood, B. (1981), *The visible library. Practical public relations for public librarians*, London, The Library Association.

Usherwood, B. (1989), *The public library as public knowledge*, London, Library Association.

Usherwood, B. (1992), 'Managing public libraries as a public service', *Public libraries journal,* 7 (6), Nov/Dec, 141–5.

Usherwood, B. (1993a), *Public library politics*, London, Library Association Publishing.

Usherwood, B. (1993b), *The Library service and leisure activities (Information UK Outlooks No 2)*, London, Library Information Technology Centre.

Usherwood, B. and Vessey, S. (1988), 'Public library education – the decline of a discipline', *Public library journal,* 3 (2), March/April, 25–9.

Van Riel, R. (ed.) (1992), *Reading the future: a place for literature in public libraries*, London, Arts Council.

Wagner, G. S. (1992), *Public libraries as agents of communication. A semiotic analysis*, Metuchen, Scarecrow Press.

Waldegrave, W. (1992), Speech to the Institute of Directors, 20 July, Cabinet Office 13/92.

Walker, D. (1994), 'The writing on the wall', *The Times*, 5 May,14.

Walker, G. (1994), *Enabling or disabling? The voluntary contract tendering of Brent Council's library service*, London, Graham Walker.

Wallis, M. (1993), *The organisational health check, East Sussex library service, the final report and recommendations*, Sussex, University of Brighton.

Walsh, K. (1992), 'Quality contracts and care', *Contracting in or out?*, Spring, 4.

Walsh, K. (1995), *Public service and market mechanisms. Competition, contracting and the new public management*, Basingstoke, Macmillan.

Wares, C. (1989), 'Paying attention to politicians', paper given to Library Association seminar, 17 March 1989. Mimeo (copy from author).

Waverley Borough Council (1996), *Public consultation exercise on the Waverley Borough Council Revenue Budget* 1996/97 Waverley Borough Council. Surrey Social and Market Research Ltd.

Weaver, F. S. and Weaver, S. A. (1979), 'For public libraries the poor pay more', *Library journal*, **104** (3), 352–5.

Welsh reorganisation (1996), 'New authorities take shape', *Library Association record*, **98** (5), 229.

White, G. and Hutchinson, B. (1996), 'Local government', in Farnham, D. and Horton, S., *Managing people in the public services*, Basingstoke, Macmillan.

White, H. S. (1985), 'The use and misuses of library user studies', *Library journal*, **110** (20), 70–1.

White, L. J. (1983), *The public library in the 1980s*, Lexington, D. C. Heath & Co.

Whitehorne, K. (1995), 'The book stops here', *The Observer review*, 22 October.

Whitley, R. (1989), 'On the nature of managerial tasks; their distinguishing characteristics and organisation', *Journal of management studies*, May.

Widdicombe Committee (1986), Committee of Inquiry into the Conduct of Local Authority business, London, HMSO (Cmnd 9799).

Wiles, E. (1996), *An investigation into the findings of the DNH public library review of England and Wales.* A study submitted in partial fulfilment of the requirements for the degree of Master of Arts in Librarianship, University of Sheffield.

Willmott, J. (1992), 'User pays: the issues', in Hazell, A. (ed.), *Access and equity: challenges in public librarianship*, Adelaide, Auslib Press.

Worrall, L. (1995), 'Managing community information resources: a developing role for UK local authorities', *Journal of industrial affairs*, **4** (2), 109–120.

Worsfold, E. (1994), Unpublished paper. Department of Information Studies, University of Sheffield.

Wrigley, L. and McKevitt, D. (1994), 'Professional ethics, government agenda and differential information', in McKevitt, D. and Lawton, A. (eds.) (1994) *Public sector management. Theory, critique and practice*, London, Sage, in association with the Open University.

Yates, J. (1983), 'When will the players get involved?', *Health and social service journal*, 1111–2.

Index